THE VIRUS CREATION LABS

A Journey into the Underground

By George Smith, Ph.D.

American Eagle Publications, Inc.
Post Office Box 41401
Tucson, Arizona 85717
—1994—

10 9 8 7 6 5 4 3 2 1

Library of Congress Cataloging-In-Publication data:

Smith, George, 1956-
    The virus creation labs : a journey into the underground / by George Smith.
                  p.   cm.
    Includes bibliographical references.
    ISBN 0-929408-09-8 ; $12.95
    1. Computer viruses. 2. Computer crimes.
I. Title.
QA76.76.C68S63   1994
005.8--dc20
                              94-42777
                                CIP

Introduction

"The current United States can be defined as an immense accumulation of not terribly acute or attentive people obliged to operate a uniquely complex technology, which, all other things being equal, always wins. No wonder error and embarrassment lurk everywhere, and no wonder cover-up and bragging have become the favored national style."

—Paul Fussell in *BAD*, 1991[1]

This book probably wouldn't exist without the great techno-white elephant of 1991-92, the Michelangelo computer virus. As I'll get into, the Michelangelo affair was the apotheosis of Paul Fussell's America: an immense accumulation of not terribly acute or attentive people were beaten repeatedly over the head by the cudgel of poorly understood computer technology. Although the Michelangelo virus was real, the nation's PCs were not about to lose their datastores to it during the months leading up to March 6, 1992, at least not in any noticeable way.

Most Americans seemed to figure this out instinctively—after the fact. Skeptics and some computer industry insiders certainly knew in February the virus would be a bust. But you never would have suspected as much from the panicked cries of software vendors and assorted experts in the computer press and mass media

---

1 Paul Fussel, *BAD, or the Dumbing of America*, Summit Books, 1991.

who predicted significant computer calamity on March 6. Predictably, error and embarrassment there were aplenty after the sixth when less successful vendors than John McAfee turned on the anti-virus software developer and blamed him for manufacturing the crisis. Bragging was in no short supply, either. *USA Today*'s technology writer, John Schneidawind, insisted during an interview that "Everyone's PCs would have crashed" if the press hadn't sounded the alarm in a timely manner.

Schneidawind attempted to cover himself in glory by comparing the Michelangelo virus threat to the menace of the BCCI bank scandal. He weirdly maintained that since the press took a hit for being asleep at the wheel on BCCI, it wasn't going to happen again with the Michelangelo computer virus. All the foolishness was summed up by Carl Jensen, a journalism professor and media critic at Sonoma State in California, who dubbed Michelangelo one of the "junk food news stories" of 1992 in the annual *Project Censored* report, "The News That Didn't Make The News—And Why."[2]

The Michelangelo debacle ignited a keen interest in me to find out what, precisely, computer viruses were, how they worked, and better yet, who was writing them. It sent me down the trail to the rim of cyberspace in search of people who, perhaps not surprisingly, turned out to be pretty much like most Americans, except with an order of magnitude greater interest in the inner workings of the desktop personal computer. Like most of us, there wasn't a nobleman in the lot—and there were none among the ranks of the anti-virus software developers and security consultants who consider themselves the gatekeepers at a fantasy wall of their own construction erected between the Wild West of cyberspace and the mannered, sterile environment of safe home and business computing.

The story of computer viruses is also a story at the apex of the vaunted age of information, its denizens mythical outriders in the new land of Nod—Information Superhighway, that country named by Vice President Albert Gore and too many futurologists to mention.

---

2 Carl Jensen, *CENSORED: The News that Didn't Make the News—and Why*, Shelburne Press, 1993.

However, this country isn't much like the pretty pictures painted in the mainstream media, where ill-defined riches and information screaming for freedom reward the quick, the clever or the unorthodox mind armed merely with a telephone line and a computer. It is, instead, a country that defines the meaning of information glut—data, data everywhere but not a thought to think. It is a world where it's clear that pushing packets of information from point A to point Z in stupefying quantity is of little benefit to anyone except those in position to place press releases as media stories-of-the-day. Those who think the United States is on the verge of creating a new utopia where the national product, currency and sole means of reward is data would do well to pay attention.

The virus programmers, the security consultants, and the anti-virus software entrepreneurs in *The Virus Creation Labs* all exist side-by-side in this new land of Nod. They're on and within the Internet, on your neighborhood bulletin board system, and chatting with anyone who will listen on commercial ventures like Prodigy. Consider Little Loc, a San Diego teen and programmer savant of Satan Bug, declaiming on Prodigy to a bemused, uncomprehending audience about the undetectability of his virus which would eventually take down Secret Service computers. This world has Fagins, too. You'll read of John Buchanan, who walked both sides of the line, sharing counsel with anti-virus software developers, security consultants and virus programmers alike while mass-producing viruses with hacker software toolkits and selling a huge library of them to anyone with the right cash. You'll meet the big egos, too, like strange Dr. Alan Solomon, an English programmer who compared himself to Winston Churchill while collecting intelligence on hackers and passing it on to New Scotland Yard in hopes of having them arrested. You'll meet Nowhere Man, the author of the original Virus Creation Laboratory, and read of the elusive members of Phalcon/SKISM, a hacking group which perfected the "art" of object-oriented virus programming while pumping out the electronic magazine known as *40Hex*. You'll read of petty crooks and bands of computer hobbyists who took seriously the idea of creating the equivalent of the world's largest electronic monuments to digital nothing, the virus exchange bulletin board system.

Like the on-line community today, the characters in *The Virus Creation Labs* have little real interest in the revitalization of democracy or any other high-minded ideals frequently cited as benefits of electronic interconnectivity, unless you consider the mindless accumulation of binary data a socially invigorating development. More often you'll find relentless hucksterism, witless gossip masquerading as reason, corrosive vulgarity, petty vendettas, dirty tricks and routine invasions of personal privacy. If *The Virus Creations Labs* is a look at a new world, you'll find it bears close resemblance to the old one, only events zip by faster and with more unpredictable ferocity.

There will, of course, be a number of people who hate *The Virus Creation Labs*. I'm going to paraphrase a small bit from Robert X. Cringely's great book, *Accidental Empires*, to describe them.

There are people in *The Virus Creation Labs* who will hate being in it at all, or will dislike the way their part plays out.

And there are those who feel they should be in this book and aren't, either because I didn't feel like interviewing them or, for one reason or another, weren't important to the story. They will hate *The Virus Creation Labs* because they're jealous of the people who are mentioned.

Last, there will be a group of technically-minded nerds who know that only their explanation of how the Dark Avenger Mutation Engine, or some similar thing, generates its 5 skillion possible permutations, is valid. They'll hate this book because it's not dry enough or has a pointed tone which they find annoying. Forget them. *The Virus Creation Labs* is for readers who don't know and don't care about the serial number engraved on the rubber feet of their new PC.

Michelangelo and the Media

"As predicted, the dread Michelangelo virus erupts, wreaking untold havoc on an estimated one computer belonging to Rose Deegle, of Rochester, N.Y., whose Christmas card list is nearly wiped out."

—*Dave Barry*[1]

In early 1992 the Michelangelo virus went into history as one of the greatest "Chicken Little" technology stories of all time. "A master of disaster" was what *The Houston Chronicle* called the virus. The sky was going to cave in on IBM-compatible personal computers worldwide.

Lurid stories in *The New York Times*, *USA Today*, *The San Jose Mercury News* and other publications repeated the same thing. A bad trip—electronic doom via the corruption of your computer's data—was coming. On Prodigy, an on-line news and entertainment service popular for its blocky graphics and relentless shop-until-you-drop advertising, yuppies who used personal computers predominantly for gaming, miscellaneous time-wasting, electronic mail and checkbook balancing were in an uproar. Every night Prodigy's special interest and hobby forums would fill up with

---

1 From Pulitzer prize-winning humorist Dave Barry's year-end wrap up of world events. *The Miami Herald*, December 28, 1992.

countless messages on Michelangelo. Do I have it? If I do have it, how do I get rid of it? What is a virus, anyway?

Leading Edge had shipped 500 computers with the hard drives contaminated with Michelangelo.[2] Vance Cook of Access Software showed up to post a message that the company had shipped Michelangelo-infected 5.25" floppy disks in one of its add-on modules to the popular computer golf simulation, *Barton Creek*. The virus was on company machines as well as PCs belonging to the diskette duplicating service Access used to produce its games. "Unfortunately, neither of our virus scan programs detected the Michelangelo virus," said Cook.[3]

However, there seemed to be little real information about Michelangelo, a small program that cloned itself by writing its operating orders to the area known as the master boot record on computer hard drives and the boot sector on floppy diskettes. To those who knew little of their computers, this was meaningless. What counted for them was that on March 6, Michelangelo—if your computer had a copy—would wake up and scribble electronic gobble over a great deal of the computer's hard disk. Games, check-book balancing programs, Prodigy software, the unfinished great American novel, electronic resumes and funny letters to family members, clients and creditors could all be gone. *Poooft*. It sounded like very serious business.

The mass fear was a symptom of information overload. News was flooding into the media and the on-line networks in such volumes that no one seemed able to weigh if it was accurate or complete garbage. Good judgment was paralyzed. That being the case, hysteria reigned.

Into the vacuum stepped anti-virus software vendors like McAfee Associates and Symantec. John McAfee had a kind of magnetic attraction for the press. He spoke in rational tones. He gave great quotes and seemed to make sense. He had the what, when, where, who, why and plenty of numbers. Better, he had the cure: His SCAN software, which found the virus, and CLEAN,

---

2 "Who's been affected", *USA Today*, March 4, 1992.
3 Public post by Vance Cook, Access Software, in the Prodigy Service's PC Club Special Interest Group. Subject: Links Parton Creek Virus, February 14, 1992.

which removed it. Both were easy to get hold of. Both were prime examples of shareware—software cast upon the electronic winds of the emerging bulletin board system nation. If there was a bulletin board system in your town and you knew its phone number, odds where you could call it with your computer and copy editions of SCAN and CLEAN to your home system. You could pay for them later. What a deal! The story was computer technology, it was cutting edge, it was dangerous!

Symantec, manufacturer of the Norton Anti-virus software, was as magnanimous as McAfee. The company made a special "teaser" edition of the full Norton Anti-virus package. It would detect Michelangelo free and you could download it from Prodigy and Compuserve. The software looked pretty while it worked. It whirled and flashed and scanned the whole hard disk in minutes even though it only had to look in one place to find Michelangelo, a process which actually should have taken only a small fraction of a second. Symantec backed it up with a big advertising campaign. McAfee Associates had a presence on Compuserve, too—its own forum—which acted as a server for McAfee shareware. Although the on-line help for Michelangelo-worried customers seemed community-spirited, it wasn't. Compuserve made $100,000 in on-line charges from the McAfee forum during the days leading up to March 6, according to an April story in Long Island's *Newsday*.[4]

Some anti-virus software developers were peeved by the hysteria surrounding Michelangelo. Pam Kane, president of a small company called Panda Systems located near Wilmington, Delaware, which also programed anti-virus software, was resident on Prodigy and posted messages from time to time proclaiming the whole thing royal bunk—a cynical move by McAfee and others to gain as much notoriety and sell as much merchandise as possible. She grumbled over a particularly ridiculous figure fed to the Reuters news service by Klaus Brunnstein, a German academic and member of the Computer Anti-virus Research Organization, a self-appointed group of software developers and hobbyists similar to John McAfee's Computer Virus Information Association.

---

4 Joshua Quittner, "Are computer viruses running rampant, or is John McAfee's antivirus campaign running amok?", Long Island Newsday, April 15, 1992.

Brunnstein insisted 25 percent of all computers in the U.S. were infected. It was a ridiculous claim, but true or not, the hype was working.

By March 5, the Associated Press was in full cry. Michelangelo was "a mugger hiding in a closet," it said, waiting to ambush your computer.[5] Anti-virus software sales were going through the roof as manufacturers flooded computer magazines and commercial networks with promotions.

The AP quoted Lee Rock, an employee of Egghead Software in Boston: "We are utterly, completely, totally sold out . . . The media whipped people into a frenzy and they are storming the gates."

AP checked in Dallas, too. CompUSA superstore shelves were empty of anti-virus software.

"The virus problem is going to get worse and worse and worse," the news service quoted computer security consultant Winn Schwartau as saying. Schwartau had just written a book called *Terminal Compromise*,[6] a fiction about computer terrorists waging cybernetic war on the United States.

Although information on Michelangelo was all of the "he said/she said" variety, with no verifiable data or copies of the virus to examine, panic reigned in many quarters. At *The Morning Call* newspaper in Allentown, Pennsylvania, employees engaged in a nutty spasm of activity backing up their MacIntosh-based network even though Michelangelo only affected IBM-compatible machines. I had written a short piece on the virus scare on February 25 for the same newspaper. I couldn't find much on Michelangelo that seemed worth publishing except the Leading Edge, Da Vinci Systems and Access Software infection notices and a few phone numbers of anti-virus software developers. A warning had also arrived claiming that a different virus, called the Computer Ogre, had contaminated diskettes which had come with the Trident SVGA video card, so I added that and some basics on what

---

5 Bart Ziegler, "Computer users brace for Michelangelo virus", *Associated Press*, March 5, 1992.

6 Winn Schwartau, *Terminal Compromise*, Inter.Pact Press, 1991.

computer viruses were and where they were thought to come from—unknown hackers. After the story ran, the phone rang. On the other end was the mother of a student at a local high school. She said her son had asked her to call because he had recently purchased the Trident SVGA video card for his PC. He wanted to know what the Computer Ogre did.

The Computer Ogre was quite annoying, I told her. Like Michelangelo, it infected the hard drive's boot record and the boot sector of floppy diskettes. Worse, if the computer was left on for over 48 hours, the Ogre virus would activate and begin encrypting the contents of the hard disk. It would let you know when this was happening by displaying the message, *"Disk Killer—Version 1.0 by Ogre Software, 04/01/1989. Warning!! Don't turn off the computer while Disk Killer is Processing!"* It was unlikely that anyone in the region would have a program capable of reversing the end result of the Ogre's meddling, so the PC would effectively be left with its data only so much electronic trash, I said. She thought this sounded bad so I asked her to have her son call me when back. Curiously, there were no calls from anyone who thought they had the Michelangelo virus.

Later in the afternoon, Tim Caton, the student, phoned. Caton, a sophomore, was unique amid all the people running around panicked. He wasn't rattled about the possibility of the Computer Ogre messing up his data. He just wanted to know what should be done next. Caton informed me he was something of a nut for computers and ran a bulletin board system out of his bedroom. He thought it would be no trouble to dig up some anti-virus shareware and take a look at what was going on, virus-wise, on his computer. However, he could no longer remember if he had started his PC from the Trident video card utility diskette. This was important because it would have been the only way the Ogre virus could have spread onto his system. So he wanted to check, just in case.

Caton was talking on the phone while he called another bulletin board system in Allentown. Soon he had a copy of John McAfee's ubiquitous SCAN program. It wasn't clear whether Caton had the Ogre virus. His PC appeared clean and he couldn't find the original diskette which came with his Trident video card. McAfee's program did, however, inform him he had a different virus called Black Monday, attached to one text file. Viruses don't normally copy themselves into text files and they can't spread themselves from them, so this was puzzling—a good example of what has become known as the *false positive*—an instance when anti-virus software tells you of the existence of a virus that isn't really there. It wasn't even critical that the file be examined for a virus. Unless it was absolutely essential, you could just throw it away. I advised Caton to forget about Black Monday but to give me a call if any of his friends actually found a copy of Michelangelo on their machines at home, school or work.

Newspapers around the country continued to run headlines in the next few days warning of imminent disaster. "Thousands of PCs could crash Friday," said *USA Today*.[7] "Deadly Virus Set to Wreak Havoc Tomorrow," said *The Washington Post*.[8] "Paint It Scary," said the *Los Angeles Times*.[9]

On March 6, most everyone realized they'd been had. However, weeks after M-day, many antiviral software vendors and some reporters still insisted the coverage had prevented thousands of computers from losing data. John Schneidawind of *USA Today* said "everyone's PCs would have crashed" had the media not paid much attention to Michelangelo.[10]

The San Jose Mercury News—the Silicon Valley's newspaper of choice—credited the publicity with saving the day. John McAfee said the press deserved a medal. Of course, he profited from the widespread panic.

Overnight, McAfee, one of the nation's leading antiviral software manufacturers and founder and chairman of his own "nonprofit" Computer Virus Industry Association (CVIA) almost cornered the market in the United States, building up a presence that would show him in control of 70 percent of all sales in 1994, when most other competitors who had benefited in 1992 had fallen

---

7 John Schneidawind, "Thousands of PCs could crash Friday: Damages could amount to millions of dollars", *USA Today*, March 4, 1992.

8 John Burgess & Sandra Sugawara, "Computer users scramble to sabotage Michelangelo; deadly virus set to wreak havoc tomorrow", *The Washington Post*, March 5, 1992.

9 Cristine Gonzales, "Paint it scary: businesses, others scramble to thwart Michelangelo PC virus", *The Los Angeles Times*, March 4, 1992.

10 George Smith, "The little virus that didn't: The press couldn't get enough of Michelangelo", *The Washington Journalism Review*, May, 1992.

by the wayside. McAfee was a colorful character, a 47-year old programmer who had earlier attempted to cash in on a kind of safe-sex club which carried a registry of HIV-negative swingers interested in meeting each other in an on-line computer database in the Silicon Valley.[11] When in an ebullient mood, he would talk or write about his vision of the future: one in which a McAfee Associates special team would drive around in a mobile home to supply emergency service to companies laid low by computer viruses. By February and March of 1992, McAfee's corporate licenses had increased by 68 percent, eventually leading to an initial public stock offering which enabled the virus scourge to pocket a cool $7 million, according to a September 1993 article in *Computer Reseller News*.[12] Since mid-1992, McAfee stock has slid, occasionally jumping erratically, perhaps appropriately peaking around March 6 of each year.

It was McAfee who told reporters in early 1992 that as many as 5 million computers—a claim which appeared to have come from another computer virus expert, Klaus Brunnstein—were at risk. McAfee said he made the projection based on a study that the virus had infected 15 percent of computers at 600 sites. The Associated Press helped send the figure around the world. After March 6, McAfee said he didn't present it the way it was reported. "I told reporters all along that estimates ranged from 50,000 to 5 million . . . I said, '50,000 to 5 million, take your pick,' and they did."[13]

One of McAfee's critics, rival security consultant Charles Rutstein, said even 50,000 was an exaggeration. Also widely quoted in newspapers, Rutstein said he told reporters early on to expect no more than 10,000 computers infected worldwide.[14] (At the time, there were more than 35 million computers in the United States alone, according to some estimates, thus making his estimated incidence of Michelangelo well below 0.01 percent.)

---

11 *Op. cit.*,, Quittner.
12 Jack Sweeney, "A tale of IPO's, viruses and investment houses", *Computer Reseller News*, September 13, 1993.
13 *Op. Cit.*, George Smith, *Washington Journalism Review*.
14 *Ibid.*

"Five million [was] just ridiculous, but the press believed it because they had no reason not to," Rutstein said in 1992. "McAfee [seemed] credible."

McAfee, for his part, retorted that Rutstein and other critics were part of "fringe groups."[15]

While many articles failed to disclose or merely mentioned in passing that McAfee's antiviral software company had sold more than 7 million copies of its Viruscan and expected revenues of more than $20 million in 1992,[16] McAfee scoffed at the idea that he or other vendors hyped the threat to generate sales. "I never contacted a single reporter, I never sent out a press release, I never wrote any articles," he said. "I was just sitting here doing my job and people started calling." He maintained at the time that the coverage of Michelangelo cost him money. "It was the worst thing for our business, short-term," he claimed. "We offer shareware [where users are trusted to pay], so we got tons of calls from non-paying customers.

"Before the media starts to crucify the antivirus community," he continued, "they should look in the mirror and see how much [of the coverage] came from their desire to make it a good story." But he added quickly, " . . . I'm [not] a press-basher."[17]

This was misleading. Although it was true McAfee's software was shareware, his company also marketed a retail anti-virus program known as ProScan and had cross-licensed the technology to IMSI and Parsons Technology, companies with versions of anti-virus software on the shelf at the time of the Michelangelo scare. And by the time the dust had cleared, McAfee Associates had received $10 million in venture capital, according to an article in *Newsday* on April 5 of the same year.[18]

USA Today's John Schneidawind tried to track Michelangelo after March 6, 1992, and found only a few thousand afflicted computers worldwide.[19] Maybe. Maybe there were some in Uru-

---

15 *Ibid.*

16 *Ibid.*

17 *Ibid.*

18 *Op. Cit.*, Quittner.

19 John Schneidawind, "Computer virus more fright than might: Michelangelo kept at bay by early detection", *USA Today*, March 9, 1992.

guay wrote USA Today, maybe some in South Africa, it was hard to tell. The estimates included 2,400 erroneously reported at the New Jersey Institute of Technology. The institute actually had only 400 computers infected with any virus; few had Michelangelo. A *Philadelphia Inquirer* reporter[20] got it wrong, said institute spokesman Paul Hassan, and it spread quickly to the Associated Press, USA Today and just about every other news service paying attention. "That was the first time I've been that close to a feeding frenzy," said Hassan in an interview.

The most crazed news effort was reserved for CNN. The cable channel staked out McAfee's offices in Santa Clara, California, on March 6, waiting to videotape a death ride of the computers that never came.[21]

Ted Koppel's *Nightline* also featured McAfee and a couple of other computer security experts. One, whose name has blessedly passed into history, babbled on crazily about being able to call up enemy military forces' computers in the Middle East and either infect or trash their systems. What this had to do with the Michelangelo virus was never explained.

The *Los Angeles Times*, which had quoted McAfee's 5 million figure on March 4,[22] carried a Reuters story three days later that reported the "Black Death" had turned out to be little more than "a common cold." AP downgraded its "mugger hiding in the closet" to a mere "electronic prank."[23]

AP Deputy Business Editor Rick Gladstone said the wire service downplayed the story after its initial reports and included comments from Charles Rutstein, who said the threat from the virus was exaggerated. "Our big oversight was to quote McAfee's 5 million figure in the beginning of the coverage but we backed off that," Gladstone said, adding that the his staff "felt somewhat vindicated" when relatively few computers were affected on March 6. "Some of us in the press were suckered," he admitted.[24]

---

20 *Op. Cit.,*, George Smith, *Washington Journalism Review.*
21 *Ibid.*
22 *Ibid.*
23 "Michelangelo virus threat downplayed", *Associatd Press*, March 6, 1992.
24 *Op. Cit.,* George Smith, *Washington Journalism Review.*

John Schneidawind continued to insist he was no dope for the software developers. "We went into this with our eyes open," he said.[25] But on March 9, in an article entitled "Computer virus more fright than might" (the subhead was a more confident "Michelangelo kept at bay by early detection"), the *USA Today* reporter chronicled his frustrations tracking the virus. He wrote that he had asked Rutstein and McAfee, again identified as the Computer Virus Industry Association chairman, to provide a working sample of Michelangelo. Both declined. "It'd be like giving him a biological virus because he wanted to play with it," said McAfee. Rutstein wouldn't do it because passing viruses would violate his code of ethics, he said. Schneidawind eventually tracked down a copy and tried to get it to infect a computer in the office. Michelangelo was reluctant. It wouldn't properly infect 3.5" diskettes—rendering them unreadable—-a property which has hastened it toward extinction in 1994. McAfee was also "reluctant to divulge the names of companies struck by the virus," according to Reuters.

Much later, in an interview that appeared in the *Washington Journalism Review*[26], McAfee estimated that only 10,000 systems were stricken worldwide on March 6, 1992, a number he said was derived by counting the number of calls he received from victims and guessing arbitrarily that they constituted five percent of the total.

Schneidawind agreed that the statistics were inflated, but rationalized that this was for the greater good anyway. He compared the Michelangelo story to the BCCI bank scam. "The estimates may have been overblown, but no one knew for sure until the 6th," he insisted. "Consider the BCCI scandal, where everyone faulted the press for not being there. I'd rather err on the side of caution."[27]

However, Schneidawind exaggerated again for his audience in a sidebar to a March 9 article in *USA Today* which listed other computer pests poised to strike in March. Supplied by yet another antiviral software vendor, Fifth Generation Systems in Baton Rouge, La., the list did not reveal that most of the bugs were either

---

25 *Ibid.*
26 *Ibid.*
27 *Ibid.*

variants of the same common virus—known as "Jerusalem"—or rare types, perhaps, found only in eastern Europe. Like many others, the story did not make clear that every week of the year is filled with trigger dates for numerous viruses, yet the world's microcomputers do not simultaneously come crashing down. On March 6, Michael Rogers and Bob Cohn of *Newsweek* offered a postmortem to Michelangelo that warned readers to "beware the next round of computer viruses," including the Maltese Amoeba and "the scariest new virus . . . the Mutation Engine."[28] What they and others such as Ted Koppel of ABC's *Nightline* and John Fried and Michael Rozansky of the *Philadelphia Inquirer* failed to say was that the Maltese Amoeba was another elusive character, at the time active only in Ireland. And as we shall see, the original Mutation Engine viruses in 1994 have yet to make it off virus exchange bulletin boards or out of the labs of anti-virus software developers.

The pungent odor of mendacity surrounding the Michelangelo virus was even more remarkable when considering the same thing happened in March 1989, although on a slightly smaller scale!

Around that time the Dutch discovered another IBM computer virus called Datacrime. Set to go off after October 12, Datacrime would obliterate the data structures on the hard disk by performing what is known as a low level format.

In the United States, Datacrime became the featured actor in the National Institute of Standards and Technology's first National Computer Virus Alert. The press immediately dubbed it the "Columbus Day" virus even though it didn't actually do anything but multiply until Columbus Day had passed. Fortuitously, IBM was able to able to market its anti-virus software on the same day NIST issued the first National Computer Virus Alert. Not a single copy of Datacrime was reported but ". . . IBM sure sold a lot of virus detection software," wrote Fred Cohen in his textbook *A Short Course on Computer Viruses.*[29]

---

28 Michael Rogers & Bob Cohn, "Not too much of a headache; but beware the next round of computer viruses!", *Newsweek*, March 16, 1992.

29 Frederick B. Cohen, *A Short Course on Computer Viruses, Second Edition*, John Wiley & Sons, 1994.

William Arnold, part of IBM's antivirus development project, bristled at Cohen's statement. IBM's virus scanner had been an in-house project for some time prior to Datacrime. The company, explained Arnold, was in a good position to supply it to consumers "since customers were in a genuine, if misguided, press-fed panic."[30]

"It was made available at a very low price; $35 for a 'per-enterprise' license, payable on, basically, an honor system," added Arnold, who conceded that many copies of the software were distributed but that "IBM most certainly did not make piles of money on it."

But how did any of this happen? What drove this press frenzy about computer viruses?

What many people looking in from the outside don't know is that journalists don't work in a void. It's rare that you'll run into an I. F. Stone-type stubbornly refusing to hobnob with subjects of stories while on or off the beat. Instead, reporters cultivate relationships. Some go to functions, conventions and press parties and they do a lot of . . . shmoozing. Shmoozing is an effective way to ensure plenty of quick story ideas and good quotes. Shmoozing—or networking as the flacks who abuse it prefer—is a tailor-made antidote for baffling, fast moving stories in the age of information. It provides a quick fix for science and technology writers who are just as stumblebum with computers, research or simple arithmetic as the average Joe in the cheap seats. Shmoozing is non-technical, uncomplicated and people oriented. For reporters, these are pluses. Without shmoozing, or networking, a technology reporter is thrown back onto his wits and might be expected to know a little about something like computer viruses, or be able to educate himself quickly without resorting to poorly chosen experts. In early 1992, who knew anything about computer viruses? Not Ted Koppel or his assistants, not McNeil or Lehrer, not CNN, not USA Today, not Associated Press, not anyone with their hands on the wheel of a major media outlet. And the story swept over them and blew everyone away.

---

30 William Arnold, IBM Antivirus Group, a public post in the National Computer Security Association's Special Interest Group on Compuserve. Message thread: Press releases and viruses, June 17, 1994.

John Schneidawind explained it this way. Years earlier, he said, while he was working for the *San Jose Mercury News*, John McAfee was always available to explain developments in the computer industry. There was a sense, said Schneidawind, that "we owed him."[31] See? That's the power of shmoozing.

Back in Allentown, Pa., Michelangelo was a no-show, too. Tim Caton still hadn't been able to find anyone from local bulletin board systems who had actually seen a case of infection.

The Morning Call newspaper reported no cases of Michelangelo except for "about six" at Lehigh University in Bethlehem, Pa., according to a computer consultant, Binod Taterway, who worked there. Lehigh University employees, presumably, would be able to recognize computer viruses since Fred Cohen, the University of Southern California graduate given the credit in 1983 for coining the term computer virus, had been a member of its faculty in 1987. This was the same year the school discovered the Lehigh virus, a program that infected only the command shell of IBM-compatibles and mangled data on students' floppy diskettes almost immediately—at the rate of about 500 a day, loaned from the university library system—ensuring that it was quite noticeable.[32] Although the Lehigh virus was little more than a trivial pest, it gained quite a bit of publicity for the school and resulted in the formation of a newsgroup on the Internet called comp.virus where computer virus researchers and anti-virus software developers still gossip and bicker among each other over who is smarter or whose software is the best.

Elsewhere in the Allentown area, John Heinrichs, the director of computing services for Lehigh County, rasped, "I don't think anyone will be affected [by Michelangelo]. Personally, I think it's a hoax."

What Michelangelo did achieve was the solidification of the corporate visibility of McAfee Associates. David Stang, another computer security consultant who at the time was working with Charles Rutstein, parroted other software vendors less successful

---

31 *Op. Cit.,*, George Smith, *Washington Journalism Review.*
32 *Op. Cit.,* Cohen.

than McAfee in March 1992 by calling the scare nothing but vendor-created hysteria.

As much as a year later, Pam Kane was still letting McAfee have it, this time blind-siding him in the July 5, 1993 issue of *The New York Times*:

"Just a couple of years ago, one anti-virus product developer created [demand for his product] at will with trumped-up and wildly exaggerated prognostications about what a new virus was going to do and when it was going to do it. Remember Michelangelo?"

It's a venal pattern repeated over and over: Anti-virus software manufacturers and security consultants carping at each other and conducting back-stabbing negative publicity campaigns in the computer or mainstream press, complicated by the entrenched practice within computer industry publishing houses allowing corporate heads or their catspaws to write books and reviews focused on their merchandise. These tricks tend to be hidden behind mock concern over high-tech petty atrocities usually perpetrated by mysterious, unseen computer vandals or hackers. Like many hardscrabble businessmen vying for commercial advantage in an increasingly confined arena dominated by one company, such tactics grant them all the charm and panache of a 60-pound bag of money-mad cockroaches.

On the Slab at Cryptic Morgue

After Michelangelo, with much unsettled in my mind except for the stone reality of media and software manufacturer-generated lies, it was necessary to find and examine some computer viruses, the more the better.

There were a couple of avenues which looked promising. One involved making a phone call to Mark Ludwig, an author living in Tucson, Arizona, who had just written *The Little Black Book of Computer Viruses*. Ludwig had sent around quite a few press releases and was easy to get hold of, so I told him I would review his book for the newspaper if he would send me a copy. He agreed to mail it.

In the meantime, the high school student mentioned earlier, Tim Caton, had managed to find a couple of viruses. Actually, he'd found one virus—called Jerusalem—in two infected files which a peer had consented to part with. Caton said he had to promise the fellow that he wouldn't pass on his name. The donor ran his own bulletin board system in eastern Pennsylvania and if it got out that he had a few viruses on hand his name would be mud, he claimed; such was the stigma attached to the programs.

The Jerusalem virus turned out to be rather boring. I began working with it on my PC. It would hook itself into the computer's memory when executed and wait for you to load other programs. When you did, it would add itself to them in the background—rather quickly, I might add. After the virus had been active for about

30 minutes, a small black rectangular box would show up in the lower corner of the computer's screen. When this occurred, the Jerusalem virus slowed the system down by tieing a hardware timer interrupt on the machine into a wasteful loop. As a result, the infected computer ran a little more jerkily than usual. Although I felt Jerusalem was basically harmless, it wasn't much of a stretch to see how humorless corporate suits or people who already hated and feared PCs would be undone if it should find its way to them. I tried to imagine how events might unfold if Jerusalem had infected the few IBM computers at the local newspaper. It was an ugly picture.

The copy of the Jerusalem virus that Caton had passed on had come in an archive that also contained an advertisement for another bulletin board system called Cryptic Morgue. A phone number was included - the area code was in Texas.

Caton explained to me that this was a very special place—probably "elite." "Elite" systems were where hackers hung out and traded secrets. He had just started his own bulletin board system, called Dark Coffin, and was in an underground publicity war with rivals in Lehigh County over who was most "elite." In Lehigh County, "elite" didn't have much to do with actual computer hacking, but everything to do with software piracy. The more pirated software you had on your BBS, the more obscure and user-hostile your BBS software, the more "elite" you were. If you were the most "elite" of the "elite," your phone was busy all the time and you could assign your system a magic password which only sycophants were privy to. To enter the most "elite" system, the uninitiated would have to call, type in answers to lengthy questionnaires filled with rude and crazy demands and wait for the system's coterie of yes-men to give the digital thumbs up or down. Offering bribes, like newly pirated games or money, was a way of greasing the wheels, too.

The biggest "elite" system in the Lehigh Valley, Marvel Universe, a pirate board operated by a Lehigh University computer science graduate student, had the Dark Coffin and everyone else beat in the publicity war. Marvel Universe was the place to be. It had all the best "warez"[1]—the most up-to-date pirated software. Because it was exclusive, the system had users who were always trying to maximize their time on it. To this end, Caton had found a hacker tool to penetrate the security on Marvel Universe. He also thought it would be an advantage while collecting computer viruses. It was called a "leech protocol" and it certainly did come in handy.

The leech protocol, explained Caton, circumvented the normal accounting system on a BBS devoted to software piracy. Normally, the manager—or sysop—of the system would grant you a certain number of digital points, either in exchange for money or bartered software. The BBS would then dispense the software you wanted, metering your points in the process. When you ran out of points, it was either time to cough up more cash or contribute more pirated software. However, the leech protocol deceived the BBS system while it was sending the software you had selected. Just as the copy of the pirated software landed in your computer and before your PC sent a message of confirmation to the sending BBS, the leech protocol would spring into action and transmit a fake error. The fake error fooled the sending BBS software into thinking that the transaction had failed. Generously, when this happened, the system would not deduct the cost of the software from your account. With the leech protocol, you could spend as much time as you liked— until the BBS manager noticed what you were doing—ripping the system off and accumulating pirated "warez" without exhausting the points on your account. This trick is rather shopworn now, but at the time it was quite novel.

Caton had called the Cryptic Morgue in Euless, Texas, and the system had a few hundred viruses. But, there was a catch. Cryptic Morgue had a tough policy. You had to upload a virus they didn't have to accumulate some points so that you could download viruses from its restricted areas. Cryptic Morgue also specialized in pirated games, so it must have seemed a small stretch for the system's managers to extend the usual pirate metering system to computer viruses. Jerusalem virus wouldn't fly, said Caton. Cryptic Morgue already had copies of Jerusalem virus up the wazoo.

However, Mark Ludwig's *Little Black Book of Computer Viruses* had just arrived in the mail, providing the answer. The book contained the source code—the printed instructions which make up computer programs—for four viruses. The instructions were in

---

1 Pirated software, that is.

what is known as assembly language, even more cryptic to most people only passingly familiar with computers than more popular high level computer programming languages like C or Pascal. But by typing the assembly instructions laboriously to a text file using any word processor, it was just possible to get them into a form which could be compiled into working computer viruses by just about anyone with the stock software on a home computer. One of these viruses, called TIMID, seemed like a logical choice to experiment with. As far as names went, TIMID was apt. TIMID told you what program it was infecting when you executed it and refused to infect more than one at a time. It restricted itself to the simplest of programs, known as .COM executables, effectively cutting its prospective hosts on any PC to much less than half the number targeted by more infectious computer viruses. And it confined itself to a single directory, curbing its reach within the system.

After a little study, the assembly language instructions of TIMID didn't seem all that hard to understand, so I thought I would jazz up the virus by adding a segment of code which made all the characters on a computer's video display drop to the bottom line. The effect lasted for quite a long time before it gave control back to the user and was, therefore, quite exasperating. I dropped it into TIMID so that it would occur whenever the virus ran out of programs to infect.

This was even simpler to do than it sounded. Mark Ludwig had included a strategy for altering TIMID virus in his book. It looked like this:

```
call FIND_FILE ;virus searches for a file to infect
jnz DESTROY    ;if no program found, do destructive
               ;code—in my case, drop letters to
               ;bottom of screen
call INFECT    ;virus found a program, so infect it
EXIT_VIRUS:
```

So now I had a modified version of the TIMID virus, which I renamed DROPSY. I showed it to my wife who knew nothing of computers. She laughed. Boy, was I a super hacker. In about 30 minutes I had just done what the great majority of virus programmers do: cobble a silly change into an existing virus and rename it. DROPSY would certainly suffice as digital currency at the Cryptic Morgue.

I decided to call Cryptic Morgue, offer them a copy of DROPSY as trade, and establish an account. When I found other viruses I wanted to take a look at, I would use the leech protocol to obtain them. It was a good plan and it worked just like that.

You may have noticed this is pretty prosaic compared to the images most people have of computer hackers and shady doings in the underground. Thank the major media for that. To be sure, there are hackers who can invade systems all along the Internet by exploiting obscure flaws in complex software, steal telephone service to just about anywhere, and pathologically root through shopping mall garbage cans for discarded credit card invoices and system passwords scribbled on post-it notes. But they have only a tangential relationship to the vast unsophisticated majority of the so-called virus underground. In fact, calling the Cryptic Morgue to bribe its sysops out of a few viruses could be called "lame," in hacker-speak.

To get into the Cryptic Morgue I had to write the usual introductory letter at the system's front door. I filled it with material from Mark Ludwig's book on viruses which I knew they wouldn't understand at all. It's a good rule of thumb in the computer underground that when confronted with this kind of situation, elaborate stories couched in the correct jargon and designed to sail right over the head of your audience work best. This is a horribly cynical observation, but true. Like many average Americans, people in cyberspace are not very good at being skeptics.

The Cryptic Morgue had a copy of the Mutation Engine which *Newsweek* reporters had mentioned in hysterical tones on March 6.[2] I thought this was rather amusing. High school kids running a pirate bulletin board system in Texas had access to "the scariest new virus . . . the Mutation Engine," but *Newsweek's* vaunted information-gathering apparatus didn't.

And the Mutation Engine wasn't a virus. The Mutation Engine, or MtE for short, was a segment of code which provided any computer virus that used it with intensely variable encryption.

---

2 Michael Robers & Bob Cohn, "Not too much of a headache; but beware the next round of computer viruses!", *Newsweek*, March 16, 1992.

Encryption code garbles virus instructions so that they look like binary nonsense attached to the host program. In general, the only part of the virus that must remain constant is the decryptor, a small stub of code which an encrypted virus uses to unscramble itself when it comes time for it to do its thing. When an infected program is executed, the decryptor is the first thing to start.

The Mutation Engine went well beyond typical virus technology by providing a variable process which, when it worked correctly, produced wildly different encryptions every time the virus multiplied. The Mutation Engine also changed the nature of its decryptor by altering the quantity and diversity of nonsense data in it along with the length of the strings of computer instructions. In essence, this action made the virus appear different after every infection, making it impossible to identify a constant marker set of instructions for the virus. It was a reasonably sophisticated piece of programming which seemingly invalidated anti-virus software that looked for viruses the old-fashioned way, by poking around for rigid strings of constant instructions unique to the virus that could be used as markers.

The Mutation Engine wasn't the first piece of viral software to do this. An American programmer, Mark Washburn, wrote a series of simple viruses which neatly crystallized this idea for computer virus disguise in 1990.[3] Washburn was also playing around with developing anti-virus software as a hobby, although he wasn't the only developer who also publicly programed viruses. Washburn insisted that he cooked up the technology as a challenge to John McAfee whom, he said, flatly believed it couldn't be done. So Washburn programed this technique to prove McAfee wrong. Today it's called polymorphism, so when you hear about polymorphic viruses, now you know it was a technology invented by one programmer and would-be software developer as an intellectual test to spite a peer who was more successful.

The Mutation Engine wasn't much like the Washburn viruses but, conceptually, it was close enough for rock and roll.

3　Jan Hruska, *Computer Viruses and Anti-virus Warfare, 2nd Ed.*, Ellis-Horwood, 1992.

McAfee Associates showed the Mutation Engine to Steve Gibson—an excitable writer for the computer magazine *Infoworld*—and he panicked publicly in a May column: "It is clear that the game is forever changed," he wrote. "The sophistication of the Mutation Engine is amazing and staggering."[4] Gibson's words made great quotes, perfect for anti-virus software press releases. Central Point Software used the specter of the Mutation Engine in its direct advertising. McAfee Associates also used Gibson in a May 11 press release.

Vince McKiernan, a McAfee Associates vice-president, claimed, "We expect that the Mutation Engine will increase [the virus] problem exponentially for those with unprotected systems."[5] Of course, if you had a copy of McAfee Associates SCAN product, it was a different matter.

"Actually, we cracked this engine some months ago and have been shipping product capable of detecting the Mutation Engine since March," he said.

Because of the MtE's notoriety, anti-virus programmers finally started getting around to the idea of designing their scanners to detect viruses which were polymorphic. Some were better than others—Fridrik Skulason's F-Prot came to mind—and some companies, notably Central Point, never got the hang of it. The Mutation Engine could be detected using statistical methods. By carefully dissecting the program and looking at the number of variations it generated from virus to virus, it was possible for some programmers to determine a pattern in its permutation. They then rewrote their software to notice the trend unique to the Mutation Engine and red-flag it.

The existing Mutation Engine viruses, however, were a singularly tame lot. One, called Sara Gordon, was included with the Mutation Engine as a demonstrator. A sentence embedded in the virus dedicated it to Sara Gordon, a computer enthusiast living in South Bend, Indiana, who had cultured an electronic mail corre-

---

4 Steve Gibson, "Polymorphic software viruses present a daunting challenge", *InfoWorld*, April 13, 1992 and "Polymorphic viruses escape detection", *InfoWorld*, April 20, 1992.

5 McAfee Associates press release, *Dark Avenger Mutation Engine no threat to protected PCs*, May 11,1992.

spondence with the virus programmer who had written the MtE, the Dark Avenger of Bulgaria. The documentation that came with the Mutation Engine was comical. Here's a sample:

```
MuTation Engine <tm>

Version 1.00b (22-04-92)
(C) 1992 CrazySoft, Inc.
written by Mad Maniac.

****** This is a beta release meant only to be distributed to the **
****** members of Destroyers, Inc. Do not, repeat, DO NOT spread! **

1. License

You are free to include this Engine in viruses. Using it in another
ways is prohibited. You are free to give it to people that will only
use it in this way. MuTaion [sic] engine is free.
```

The documentation wrapped up with:

```
Well, that's for now. No time for more. Look at the demo virus and
other sample files included here to get an idea how can you use it. Af-
ter you include it in your virus, please check carefully if the Engine
does what you expect it to do. Feel free to experiment with it. If you
have problems using it, or have any comments or suggestions about it,
write a message to Dark Avenger at the:

Virus eXchange BBS in Sofia
Phone number: (+359)-2-20-4198
Working hours: 20:00—06:00 GMT (in the winter)
              19:00—05:00 GMT (in the summer)

The final release of the Engine should also be available at that BBS.
Remember do not pass the Engine to any others than the members of De-
stroyers, Inc.!

Greetings,
CrazySoft, Inc.
Bulgaria
```

Presumably Mr. CrazySoft/Mad Maniac/Dark Avenger was trying to cultivate a dry sense of humor in his work but it remains difficult to tell in 1994. Other virus programmers would parrot the style of the Dark Avenger's crippled English in the documentation for their own programs until it became a running joke within the computer underground. However, a wag might be led to observe that the Dark Avenger's English was better than most Americans' anyway. Not me, though.

As far as viruses went, Sara Gordon was about on a par with Mark Ludwig's TIMID. At best, it was a reluctant infector. True, the Mutation Engine made it hard to detect with anti-virus scanning software, but the virus wasn't the kind that would be going anywhere in the wild.

The only other virus at the time that utilized the Mutation Engine was called Pogue Mahone. Pogue Mahone was written by a Dutch hacker called Masud Khafir. Khafir was part of an informal bunch of virus programmers who eventually dubbed themselves Trident. He was very interested in the Mutation Engine and would later devise his own polymorphic virus tool called the Trident Polymorphic Engine, or TPE.

The appearance of the TPE, a complete replacement designed to render the MtE obsolete, revealed another flaw in the claims of anti-virus developers who insisted the Mutation Engine and its instructions made it simple for every high school computer vandal to make their own Mutation Engine viruses. The TPE, unlike the MtE, was actually documented sufficiently so that many others could use it. The MtE—by contrast—was almost unusable and as a result today there are still only a handful of Mutation Engine viruses.

Why unusable? It boiled down to this: The Mutation Engine wasn't as plug-and-play as computer security consultants complained. It was poorly explained. And it had a flaw in that it wasn't particularly "relocatable." Virus code, because of the things it's asked to do when attached to an infected file, has to be relocatable because the size of the infected program is always changing from infection to infection and the virus has to be able to perform some gymnastics in computer memory to ensure that it and its hosts continue to function properly. Any theoretical hacks—or new forms—of MtE viruses were constrained by this rigidity in its design. Contrary to Dark Avenger's expressed desire, his code was hard to use. Most hackers, when faced with it, went and designed their own engines from the ground up without worrying about such things as ease of use.

In addition, the MtE gained so much publicity every anti-virus software developer was forced to deal with it. Since virus programmers shunned making viruses that were detected even before they could be traded on bulletin boards, even relatively non-virulent crippled MtE viruses weren't an option for them. The Mutation

Engine wasn't bug free either. It was slightly unstable with the result that viruses employing it tended to behave weirdly or crash the machine when replicating. The MtE's only significance was that if virus programmers hadn't already been aware of the Mark Washburn viruses, the Engine—trumpeted by the anti-virus software developers and computer journalists—tipped them to the idea of polymorphic viruses, at which point they went and wrote their own mimics.

The Mutation Engine also inspired an absurd parallel naming convention among virus programmers. Some examples of other polymorphic virus encryptors that appeared after the MtE were the MutaGenic Agent, the Dark Angel Multiple Encryptor, the Dark Slayer Mutation Engine, the Dark Slayer Confusion Engine, and the Guns & Roses Polymorphic Engine. Get the idea?

In addition to the Mutation Engine, Cryptic Morgue had a collection of electronic documents, or on-line magazines, named *40 Hex*. *40 Hex* was a magazine written by a loose collection of hackers which called itself phalcon/SKISM[6]. Originally written by and for virus programmers to expedite the process of virus writing, it evolved over the years into a magazine also coveted by security experts and anti-virus software developers. Quite regularly, various security consultants and anti-virus software programmers would denounce others in their field who advertised its possession or claimed interest in the magazine. Ownership of *40 Hex* was always good fuel for firing some petty outrage in the computing community, which would invariably weigh in with an exaggerated amount of concerned noise-making, vitriolic condemnation and hypocritical tut-tutting in trade magazines. Judging by these outbursts, an outsider might think that *40 Hex* contained programming secrets as dangerous to civilization as the complete schematics and manufacturing plans for deuterium/tritium-boosted fission bombs with TNT equivalence in the near-megaton range.

One of the first security consultants to be blitzed by colleagues in this phenomenon was Hans Braun, the operator of a San Francisco bulletin board called COM-SEC.

---

6 An acronym for "Smark Kids Into Sick Methods".

Hans Braun distributed *40 Hex* to interested parties from COM-SEC and he wrote, "I personally believe it is helpful to know what hackers and virus writers are up to . . . Some of the information provided [in *40 Hex*] is quite sensitive and in the wrong hands could be used against you . . . The point is that it IS ALREADY in the wrong hands . . ." Braun published this in the July 1992 issue of the *National Computer Security Association News.*[7]

Braun was absolutely correct. After all, in the same time period I had collected a number of *40 Hex*es from Cryptic Morgue, a system operated by teenagers.

But in September he was blind-sided by an article in *LAN Times* entitled "Beware of the infested underground BBS."[8]

"Virus-authoring toolkits for creating rogue code are working their way into the arsenals of the nation's top computer crackers. . ." the piece began.

" . . . ironically, the legitimate BBSes are often the best sources for the cracker network. There is one BBS in San Francisco whose members are made up almost entirely of security practitioners."

Reporter Laura Didio's story went on to say COM-SEC was making *40 Hex* available to anyone—including hackers interested in programming viruses.

Actually, COM-SEC was far from the best source for *40 Hex*, as far as the computer underground was concerned. COM-SEC was much too straight a place for users who fancied boards with names like Cryptic Morgue. It was dull—far from "elite"—by hacker standards. Hans Braun used his real name, not an alias, for cryin' out loud. No, your average self-respecting underground hacker wouldn't have been caught dead on COM-SEC.

In 1994, Braun reflected on the incident which, he said, was instigated by David Stang, a security consultant who founded the International Computer Security Association in early 1992, and Alan Solomon, an Englishman who was president of S&S International in the United Kingdom, a company that manufactured anti-virus software. Braun said Stang had lectured him about the

---

7 Hans Von Braun, "*40 Hex*: underground bulletins", *National Computer Security Association News*, July-August, 1992.

8 Laura Didio, "Beware the infested underground BBS", *LAN Times*, September 14, 1992.

dangerous nature of virus code. "In his opinion, there were only a handful of people in the entire world qualified to have access to it. Of course, David Stang was one of them," said Braun.[9]

Braun said the smear job prompted other computer security experts, including Frank Tirado, an employee at the United States Department of Agriculture, to write letters of protest to *LAN Times*.[10] Eventually, the effort to tar Braun petered out and in 1994 COM-SEC still carries *40 Hex*.

"The anti-virus software industry is going through a shake-out; not everyone is successful anymore," said Braun. "It's my opinion, most of these kinds of things are really attempts to keep access to information from competitors."[11]

Have you noticed how little this has to do with virus programmers?

After using the leech protocol to gather *40 Hex* magazines from Cryptic Morgue, it was time to move on. The users at the BBS didn't trade much chat about computer viruses. In fact, they evinced little interest in them at all. Instead, another underground system beckoned. It was called The Hell Pit and the phone number was included in an advertisement bundled with the *40 Hex* magazines from Cryptic Morgue. The ad was direct:

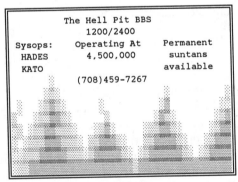

```
            The Hell Pit BBS
               1200/2400
Sysops:     Operating At      Permanent
HADES       4,500,000         suntans
KATO                          available

            (708)459-7267
```

We want your viruses!

9 Interview with Hans Von Braun, May, 1994
10 *Ibid.*
11 George Smith, "The creeping evil of people with funny names whom you will never meet", *The Crypt Newsletter*, No. 25, May, 1994.

The Hell Pit, in Wheeling, Illinois, a suburb of Chicago, made Cryptic Morgue look like the work of amateurs. It carried a mind-blowing amount of computer viruses on-line in 1992, an impression echoed by many others who were interviewed for this book. Hell Pit had created such virtual hysteria over its viruses that its reputation had leaked into books printed at home and overseas. John Dvorak had exclaimed about it in *Dvorak's Guide to PC Telecommunications.*[12] Jan Hruska, another anti-virus software developer, mentioned it in his 1992 book, *Computer Viruses and Anti-virus Warfare.* For some reason, though, he thought it was in California.

"Although the police in several countries have tried to close down virus exchange bulletin boards, this has so far been unsuccessful for a number of reasons, which range from ineffective or non-existent legislation to the difficulty in obtaining intelligence on the exact bulletin board activity," Hruska wrote.[13] Hruska made finding Hell Pit sound like a Cold War operation requiring CIA-sponsored expertise in spying and counterintelligence to get anywhere. This wasn't the case, but understandable coming from a software programmer who tended to say things like "Hackers are people analogous to drug addicts."

Although most people interested in hacking and viruses hadn't read any of these books, word of their mention had leaked into the underground and become part of cyber lore. As a result, Hell Pit was flooded with users, most of whom often seemed to "be dumber than three coats of paint," according to Hades, Hell Pit's manager. Some of these same users would sporadically become convinced Hell Pit was what was known as a "sting board," a trap run by some shadowy, always unnamed, branch of the U.S. government interested in collecting information on hackers prior to arresting them. It was a farcical claim which recurred unpredictably.

Hell Pit was home to virus programmers and hackers of all stripes. It was also visited frequently by security workers in the U.S.

---

12 John Dvorak & Nick Anis, *John Dvorak's Guide to PC Telecommunications, 2nd. Ed.*, McGraw Hill, 1992. "It's there that you can download a virus or the source code to it," wrote Dvorak of Hell Pit. "It's a new hobby, folks."

13 *Op. cit.*, Hruska.

government interested in getting information on viruses and other hacker techniques from the source. Frank Tirado, of the U.S. Department of Agriculture was one such user; Kim Clancy of the U.S. Bureau of Public Debt's Security Branch, of whom we shall read more later, was another. This was widely known on Hell Pit since the security consultants disclosed their affiliations to anyone who asked.

Sara Gordon visited Hell Pit for a time, too, at one point uploading some dummy files which resembled viruses to the system's virus library. It appeared to be an attempt to demonstrate that no one checked uploads on the system, indicating an embarrassing lack of technical competence. It created an immediate stench, making Gordon a controversial—sometimes hated, sometimes fascinating—figure to virus programmers. Many became convinced she had a crush on the Dark Avenger and, in general, suffered from a strange affection for the virus underground. Others thought she was gathering as much information as possible in order to ingratiate herself with anti-virus software manufacturers. From time to time, she would write about her escapades in security publications.

Hell Pit was also the hangout of Nowhere Man, the programmer of the Virus Creation Laboratory, a colorful menu-driven application that someone who can't even code a BASIC program could use to make a variety of simple viruses.

Generally, Hell Pit's policy was like Cryptic Morgue's. You had to upload a novel virus, get some file points, and the system would meter your access. The going rate for viruses, no exceptions, was 100 points, a nice round number which made calculations easy.

Although Hell Pit had the MtE, it did not have any viruses that used it except for Sara Gordon's namesake. Opportunity beckoned.

I was going on vacation to North Carolina's Outer Banks and I took my PC. On days when the wind blew from the Albemarle Sound west of the Banks' barrier islands, hordes of biting flies would waft in from the stagnant water to the beaches near Kitty Hawk, ensuring that everyone cowered inside. It was on one of these afternoons that I diddled with the Sara Gordon virus and the Mutation Engine until CryptLab virus was born. Like DROPSY, CryptLab was a trivial affair. I pushed and tweaked the Sara Gordon virus until it would infect more than one program at a time and add itself to non-executable computer data, ruining it in the process. I embedded a marker in it that said: "CryptLab: The select choice for your virus research needs."

CryptLab was a good introduction at Hell Pit. Surprisingly, I learned a year later that a part-time computer consultant in Southern California named Jon Rubin was using CryptLab as a demonstrator for a continuing education class on computers in Beverly Hills. CryptLab, said Rubin, got the attention of the class, mostly because it was easy to clean up and it ruined files in a manner that was graphic. Normally, each of the continuing education classes had to be instructed on how to use database and spreadsheet programs. CryptLab would mess up the data used in spreadsheets and databases, but not so thoroughly that the machine crashed. The students would start the programs, look at their neatly arranged figures and find that CryptLab had printed its own binary data over them, making the entries in the spreadsheet look like splattered nonsense. It gave the students something to talk about as well as a good picture of what the business end of a computer virus could look like. Plus you could say it was a Mutation Engine virus, which—thanks to the media—many had already heard of.

The points gained from exchanging CryptLab at Hell Pit enabled me to download Nowhere Man's Virus Creation Laboratory.

The Virus Creation Laboratory made Nowhere Man an instant sensation on Hell Pit. It maddened anti-virus software developers even though it pumped out buggy code which ensured viruses manufactured by it were more entertaining than threatening. It also ignited the curiosity of every teenage would-be hacker who heard of it. Think. If you were a disgruntled teenager with numerous real or imagined axes to grind and you had just been told of the possibility of getting a free computer program which would make something guaranteed to vex parents, teachers and other authority figures, wouldn't you want a copy? Of course you would. Movies are made from this kind of stuff.

Like so many other things in contemporary American society, the Virus Creation Laboratory was a direct result of life imitating art. Nowhere Man was a high school student, bored out of his mind by a computer teacher who—like many—was years behind his students in comprehension. Nowhere Man had been reading a book about the future, a silly thing, he said, which prophesied a computer virus-making machine.

"I started to wonder what a computer virus-making machine would look like. What would it do?" he said. So Nowhere Man went to work making his own computer virus-making machine, getting side-tracked only when a computer game called Ultima 7 hit the stores.

"The Virus Creation Laboratory got put on the shelf for a few weeks while I was playing Ultima 7," Nowhere Man laughed.

Nowhere Man's insta-virus software also set off a race among other hackers, most notably a rival programmer named Dark Angel of phalcon/SKISM, to produce superior programs which performed the same functions and then some. These virus manufacturing toolkits accelerated the creation of viruses that could be used as digital currency on BBSes. Anyone who had a "virus-making machine" could immediately begin pumping out as many trivial viruses as they desired, literally printing their own electronic version of money in underground circles. As the numbers of insta-viruses mounted, anti-virus software developers began complaining to the media about the rising tide threatening to engulf computers. They suggested laws to put virus programmers in jail and went to Congress about it.

However, the people using virus toolkits and *40 Hex* magazine to make new viruses were not the same kind of hackers that Clifford Stoll wrote about in *The Cuckoo's Egg*. These weren't foreigners or members of some exotic computer club locked in front of a PC for hours on end while sifting through government and academic mainframes from the redoubt of a satellite link. They weren't Robert Morris Jr., who unleashed the Internet worm which briefly crippled mainframes nationwide. They weren't Knight Lightning, Phiber Optik, the members of the Legion of Doom or any of the type of hackers involved in Bruce Sterling's *The Hacker Crackdown*. These were computer hobbyists who had acquired home computers much later. They had more in common with your average shmoe. They were the type of fellow not even trusted by parents to do an adequate job in the backyard with a rake and a box of pumpkin-colored plastic leaf bags.

Nevertheless, they were immediately dubbed a national menace by security consultants, who certainly knew better. Alan Solomon and David Stang, writing about the VCL in the last issue of *Virus News and Review* before it folded, declared, " . . . we can be sure that [VCL's] author is a young male, with an unpalatable level of anger and disrespect for others."[14]

"It is now time to shut down all the virus BBS's in the world, and keep them shut down," they continued. ". . . If everyone is awaiting some public outrage, let's offer it."

They were as good as their words. A coterie of anti-virus developers, including David Stang and Alan Solomon, would devote much of the rest of 1992 and 1993 to harassing mixed-up hackers and politically incorrect colleagues, fabricating their coveted "public outrage."

---

14 Alan Solomon & David Stang, "Virus Creation Laboratory: a review", *Virus News and Reviews*, July, 1992.

The Creeping Evil of People with Funny Names

The Virus Creation Laboratory put a burr under the saddle of conservatives in the computing world. Unlike most of the vaguely menacing debris washed in from the shoals of the computer underground, Virus Creation Laboratory was easy to understand and use.

It came with documentation that could be printed into a user manual. And the manual was better written than most retail software help.

"Welcome to Nowhere Man's Virus Creation Laboratory, a product to re-define the virus-writing community," it read. "No longer does one need to spend weeks writing and debugging assembly language to produce a working, competitive virus. With V.C.L. all of the work is done for you—you just choose the options and effects of the virus and it does the rest, leaving you free to experiment with different effects and concentrate on creativity. What was once a matter of hours, days, or even weeks is reduced to a few minutes in the slick V.C.L. Integrated Development Environment."

VCL was pretty, too. In 1992 that stood for a lot. Microsoft Windows hadn't quite conquered the PC world and computer magazines were still viciously knocking programmers for saddling the computing public with contorted, counter-intuitive conventions and the awful black space of bare DOS. VCL, in fact, was more user-friendly than most anti-virus software. An idiot could tinker with it.

Nowhere Man, the high school hacker from Chicago, knew that it was the look of his "virus-making machine" that would make it a hit.

"If I had made it just another command-line program, like most of the stuff from the underground, it wouldn't have gone anywhere," he said. "That was the point everyone was missing; it was supposed to look cool."

The Virus Creation Laboratory did, indeed, look cool. It had a scrolling title which made part of the interface look like a neon sign. It had a "boss key," a trick popular in computer games. If you were messing with the Virus Creation Laboratory on someone else's time—like you might with a game—you could strike the "boss key" and VCL would produce an anonymous-looking command line. It was the very picture of what a science-fiction author might envision as a "virus-making machine."

VCL's main drawback was that some of the viruses it produced weren't particularly well thought out. For example, VCL contained options for armoring its viruses. Armoring is a term programmers coined to describe coding tricks used to prevent other programmers from seeing what exactly is going on in proprietary code. In viruses, armoring is designed to foul up klutzy anti-virus researchers and security consultants. What an armored VCL virus would do was turn off the PC's keyboard when someone ran through the virus's instructions with a diagnostic tool. The only resort, once the keyboard went dead, was to restart the system and dump whatever you were working on—in this instance, the virus. Unfortunately, VCL code did not turn the keyboard back on after it was done with this trick. Of course, whenever such a virus ran, it locked the keyboard immediately, giving itself away. Like most software, VCL had at least one glaring bug.

Nowhere Man admitted he was embarrassed by it and sent out a note that users ought not to use the armoring feature if they wanted working viruses. And the VCL was limited to primitive viruses, some of which needed a little more fiddling to make it work properly. The viruses weren't sophisticated, they were easy to follow and spread only slowly. VCL also had no options for stealth—characteristics that hide viruses from anti-virus software.

VCL had other advantages, however, like support from other programmers. A hacker named Rigor Mortis had cooked up a small program that embellished one of VCL's features: the ability to make a virus that spread another virus on a system. "Rigor Mortis wasn't that great a programmer," said Nowhere Man, "but the idea was good. He really wanted to be involved in the project."

Rigor Mortis' VCL option would convert a virus or any other kind of nuisance software into data that could be utilized by a VCL virus. Then, when the VCL virus was being programed, it could be designed to piggy-back the second program across a system. In this manner, one could add more sophisticated viruses to VCL programs in one step, souping up their payload considerably. Nowhere Man also concocted a host of add-ons to work with VCL. These were called the Nowhere Utilities and their basic purpose was to provide means for disguising viruses and other software booby-traps by packing them in custom-generated fake "warez" designed as lures for the feeble-minded, gullible and avaricious in the computer underground.

Ideally, Joe Neuromancer would find one of these "fakewarez" floating around in cyberspace or have it uploaded to his system. Unable to resist running a new game, or elite hacking tool that promised to get him into the Pentagon's most secret databases, Joe would find the "fakewarez" had distressingly corrupted all the data on the BBS he was running out of his bedroom, crashing it.

The Nowhere Utilites, said Nowhere Man, were for taking down lamers.

Today, most of the VCL viruses look old. Nevertheless, there are still hackers in the computer underground grinding away making new variations on them. One of these viruses was called Olympic and it appeared—you guessed it—about the time of the 1994 Winter Olympics. Although it wasn't actually on any computers in the Olympic Village at Lillehammer, it was enough for the media that the virus had an Olympic tie-in.

Called Olympic Aid(s) by its creator, The Penetrator, it was a straightforward VCL virus made with the tools Nowhere Man had furnished to the underground in 1992.

In the documentation to his virus, The Penetrator wrote, "Hopefully the Olympics at Lillehammer is over when you read this. This virus was made only for creating fear, and some publicity."

Olympic was programed to activate on February 12 and displayed the Olympic rings along with the message: "Haakon and Kristin blew it up again . . . This time they have been fucking around with the Olympic computers and managed to infect a lot of the computers with a little tiny destructive virus . . . Now, Antonio, you can't let them runaway with this, punish the little bastards!" Then it was supposed to destroy the data residing on the hard disks of infected PCs. Haakon and Kristin were the Olympic mascots.

On Feb. 4, the Deutsche Presse-Agentur wire service claimed unnamed experts were estimating the chances that the Olympic virus would cause total data meltdown, by destroying the Olympic results-tabulating software, at 1 in 10.[1] This was insane and based solely on the supposition that if—and that was a big if—the virus was widespread on Olympic computers, the Penetrator had progra-med it to roll the digital dice before data destruction, giving users a 10 percent probability of snake eyes after February 12. Although the Olympic virus wasn't spreading anywhere, its word of mouth reputation had. The Penetrator wasn't crazy. He was crude, but he knew his audience. You can guess the rest. On February 12, the Olympic village refused to burst into flames and there was no evidence the virus had even been within 100 miles of the place.

While Virus Creation Laboratory certainly wasn't the first home virus toolkit, the straight computing community blew it so out of proportion that it acquired a symbolic identity ensuring its immortality. There had been the Virus Construction Set, a German hacker tool which produced one custom-made virus—called Manta—which you could autograph with your name or a catchy saying. And a Frenchman had attempted to market a virus-maker called GenVir as retail software. A demonstration copy was issued that didn't actually make viruses, but promised to do so for a fee. You could send the author some francs and he would send you a working copy, designed to produce viruses claimed suitable for testing the security of military systems. Eventually someone hacked the GenVir and NuKE, a virus-programming hacker group of which Nowhere Man was a member, distributed it to all takers free of charge. Both the Virus Construction Set and GenVir were virtually ignored by the U.S. hacker community, (1) because they were issued first in their native languages, only later in badly

---

1 "Viruses at Olympics", *Deutsche Presse-Agentur/Compuserve Online Today Global and Basic News Service*, February 4, 1994.

translated English; and (2), when the NuKE hacking group redistributed the GenVir, one of its programmers, an erratic, blustery virus writer who calls himself Rock Steady had altered it so that the program appeared to have one of his viruses hidden in it. Since all of Rock Steady's viruses tended to be horribly destructive, it was his misfortune that the anti-virus software used by other hackers detected GenVir as virus-infected. Knowing Rock Steady's reputation, they promptly discarded the program. The GenVir wasn't really infected by a virus, but Rock Steady, like many virus writers, couldn't resist the temptation to put his mark upon it. A segment of code from one of his viruses was close at hand and it must not have occurred to him that other software might sniff bad news once he had buried it in the GenVir. When other members of the computer underground pointed this out, Rock Steady was genuinely outraged. Brian Oblivion (named after a character in the sci-fi movie "Videodrome"), a high school student in Waco, Texas, who ran his own bulletin board system devoted to viruses, drew attention to this gaffe and was promptly excommunicated from NuKE's corner of the underground as a lamer—such were the egos of virus writers.

Although the virus underground was a good place to enjoy such comedies of errors, none of it could be seen in the mainstream press. Instead, anti-virus types would be torn between planting alarmist stories with threatening "the hackers are coming, the hackers are coming" angles and telling the truth, which was: you really didn't need their software to protect yourself from VCL because (1) You had a better chance of being hit by a car than being infected and, (2) anti-virus software didn't work that well, anyway.

On-Track Systems, a Minneapolis firm that marketed Alan Solomon's Anti-Virus Toolkit, was able to spread the word to the *San Jose Mercury News*, which told its readers in August of 1992, "the [VCL] allows would-be saboteurs with only rudimentary computer skills to manufacture freshly minted viruses at the rate of 16 an hour,"[2] which was remarkable if only for the fact that someone appeared to have timed how long it took to make them.

---

2 Tom Schmitz, "Saboteur's program ugly, lacking in sophistication", *San Jose Mercury News*, August 21, 1992.

On-Track was worried because, although the company hadn't actually found any VCL viruses, "it could . . . easily increase the number of people willing to try their hand at wreaking computer havoc." On-Track thought VCL stupid and ugly.

By December 1992, David Stang—who had demonstrated incredible flair for dealing with the computer press—had popped up in COMPUTE magazine to bang the drum about VCL.

In a short story called "Controlling The Infectious" Stang's International Computer Security Association was said to be attempting to call for legislation which would felonize virus authors, their software and publications.[3]

"Last July, a hacker calling himself Nowhere Man released version 1.00 of Virus Construction [sic] Laboratory, a slick, professional product intended to write a variety of viruses that resist debuggers . . . " said COMPUTE. Stang had written a critique of VCL in his publication, *Virus News and Reviews*,[4] which ridiculed it's code armoring bug but this wasn't passed along to readers.

"Such products," said Stang, "are destined to make today's virus problems look like 'the good ol' days.'"

The ICSA, said the article, was going to protect Americans by moving to enact laws that would encourage the capture and criminal prosecution of virus writers. It was a grandiose one-sentence plan, perfect for republication. However, the ICSA was in disarray. Its magazine, *Virus News and Reviews*, had collapsed at mid-year. Some of its field researchers and editorial advisors had jumped ship, preferring to get their information on viruses from systems like Hell Pit and Phalcon/SKISM's LandFill, a BBS located in Rockland County, New York. *VNR* contributors Jim Lipshultz of the Drug Enforcement Agency, Frank Tirado of the USDA and Baltimore Gas & Electric's Paul Melka were among the crowd that seemed to prefer talking with hackers over swallowing half-truths disseminated via the media.

None of the brouhaha surrounding VCL was lost on the segment of the hacker underground interested in viruses. One virus

---

3	"Controlling the infectious", *Compute*, December, 1992.
4	Alan Solomon & David Stang, "Virus Creation Laboratory: a review", *Virus News and Reviews*, July, 1992.

writer, Dark Angel of phalcon/SKISM, was ready to release his own virus construction kit, the PS-MPC, or phalcon/SKISM Mass-Produced Code Generator. Dark Angel, according to phalcon/SKISM's official (in his words) "mouthpiece," Dave Goldsmith, was a "programming genius."

"Five years from now," said Goldsmith, the editor of *40Hex*, "DA will really be doing something special, he's that talented. I'm sure of it."

Even anti-virus software developers used Dark Angel's work. "The magazine *Virus News International* actually plagiarized Dark Angel's history of virus toolkits in one of its issues," Goldsmith said.

Single-handedly, Dark Angel had been cranking out tutorials on virus-writing entitled the *Phunky Virus Writing Guides* and filling *40Hex* with assorted disassemblies of dangerous code and comment. The PS-MPC was going to be his crowning achievement.

The PS-MPC, he said, was dedicated to "the virus and anti-virus communities, both of which profit from [its] introduction . . ." and was inspired by VCL.

However, PS-MPC was better. It produced more sophisticated viruses—still no advanced tricks—but viruses which in 1992 worked far better than VCL programs. Dark Angel was almost schizophrenic about it. First he would praise VCL, crediting it with the germ of the idea. Then he would insult Nowhere Man, asserting that colorful, graphics-loaded programs for making viruses were for "cripples."

" . . . you, the user of the PS-MPC, are no cripple," Dark Angel ranted, "so you need no puny [Integrated Development Environment] with colorful, deluxe windows to aid you . . . Hell, port the code to the Macintosh and you can be truly crippled (although you'll have your pretty windows and icons)."

Virus toolkits were no longer for schnooks, Dark Angel implied. They weren't toys. They were only for manly men.

Like VCL, PS-MPC produced its own support industry, of sorts. Other virus writers wrote front-ends for the program so that even the "cripples" could use it. Imitation was the sincerest form of flattery in the hacker underground, too. Another virus-writing group, quizzically named Youth Against McAfee, reverse engineered the PS-MPC, threw in a dram of VCL code and repackaged it as its own virus maker, the Instant Virus Production Kit. IVP still produced PS-MPC viruses, but the names embedded in the code were different. If Dark Angel had copyrighted his software, he could have brought suit against YAM for stealing his intellectual property.

But the real master of the PS-MPC was a new virus writer who called himself Aristotle. In real life Aristotle was a student in his mid-30's named John Buchanan, who ran a bulletin board system called the Black Axis out of his home in the Virginia Beach area. Buchanan admitted from the start that he was a wretched assembly programmer, but that didn't stop him from using the PS-MPC, which enabled him to crank out a whopping 3-5 viruses per week, depending upon how he felt, throughout the second half of 1992.

"The PS-MPC revolutionized the way viruses [were] written," exclaimed Buchanan, a transplanted six-foot Texan who sounds like a dead ringer for American actor Tommy Lee Jones. "A lot of people failed to recognize this, but modular programming is an industry standard," he continued.

The PS-MPC brought "modular programming" to viruses insisted Buchanan. It was a first. "What is wrong with borrowing segments from other people's code if you're going to end up writing the same thing again? Isn't that a prime example of re-inventing the wheel? The PS-MPC was extremely helpful in teaching me . . . The code was simple, effective and easily manipulated into other . . . variations."

One of Buchanan's variations, for example, would scrunch up the type on your computer screen. Another accused John McAfee of writing the Whale virus—a German critter famous for its complexity. It was called McWhale. Yet another serenaded the victim with a few almost unrecognizable bars from a tune by Led Zeppelin. Still others displayed dirty pictures. One of these annoyed Sara Gordon—a computer hobbyist from South Bend, Indiana, who liked to mix with virus writers—to such an extent she accused Buchanan of sexual harassment by virus in the Virus News International computer security magazine.

"This virus contained a very obscene graphic of me . . ." wrote Gordon angrily in the May 1993 issue of *Virus News International*. "Because this crime was committed using the computer instead of a paint set, I am powerless."[5]

Buchanan's NewSara virus didn't actually display a picture of Sara Gordon. What it featured was a poorly-skilled computer artist's conception of a vaguely female shape flat on its back with legs spread. "Sara's Groove" was the caption the virus added to the picture as the computer pooted out a discordant melody in the background. It was the essence of vulgarity and poor taste. Naturally, everyone in the virus underground wanted a copy.

Buchanan had little idea what Sara Gordon looked like, though. What he did know was how to push her buttons. Gordon had previously had her name embedded in the first virus using the infamous Dark Avenger's Mutation Engine. Being associated with one of the world's most skilled virus writers was cool. But having your name in a stupid, completely unviable virus written by mean Texan John Buchanan was a hanging offense. NewSara was just one more example of how normally sane people could get completely spastic over computer viruses.

Finally, Buchanan designed a program called the Aristo-Hack which used the PS-MPC to make 500 new viruses in one session. The Aristo-Hack would make the hard drive churn as the whole machine rattled and shook for an hour until Buchanan's monster had programed the PS-MPC to create a veritable digital mountain of compressed electronic anti-joy. It mattered little to Buchanan that the 500 Aristo-Hack viruses were essentially 10 different variations cloned 50 times each with a net difference of about 10 bytes between them. It was 500 viruses that could be bundled and sent to anti-virus software developers who were compelled, by duty, to sort through them and document which were new and which not, which ones worked, and which ones were hexadecimal rubbish. It was 500 viruses that could be electronically sent to any chowderhead who ran a bulletin board, immediately making the system an official virus exchange.

Even though PS-MPC viruses were as easy to detect as VCL programs, the weird numbers that Aristotle was generating began to creep into press releases from software developers who would speak of the 1,500, the 2,000, the 2,500 total virus strains now in existence. Aristotle loved the controversy. It made him the center of attention among other virus writers and computer security ex-

---

5   Sara Gordon, "Information resources under attack", *Virus News International*, May 1993.

perts alike. The virus-writing group NuKE enlisted him, a decision some of its members would regret time and time again. When asked, Buchanan said he was doing it all for a thesis project for his college advisor. The research was on the virus underground. "I got an A. Ha-ha," he laughed.

However, if computing in the United States was threatened by VCL and the PS-MPC, there was still little evidence of it.

What *had* transpired was that high-quality virus disassemblies—analyzed source code—of viruses had moved onto virus exchange bulletin boards like Hell Pit and Cryptic Morgue. 40Hex magazine was publishing some of these disassemblies. But others, ironically, were the work of a collection of anti-virus researchers who detested virus exchange BBS's on the principle that they only worsened the "virus problem." In the early Nineties, as the anti-virus industry grew, various researchers had been loose with their virus analyses. Dissections of the Traceback, Icelandic, many Bulgarian viruses and others were seen as status symbols, evidence that you were, indeed, a virus expert. So, they were passed around to any who asked: students, colleagues and competitors one might be interested in doing business with in the future or anyone who might have something of value, like other new viruses, to trade. With such careless handling, it was only a short period of time before the source code wound up in the computer underground, were it was only natural for people to trade it for even more code, or the latest viruses. The availability of source code only made it easier for virus programmers to copy what had already been done into new viruses.

Vesselin Bontchev—a Bulgarian expatriate computer virus researcher working in Germany whom Fred Cohen had dubbed a "well-known . . . malicious virus defender"[6]—had written virus disassemblies which could be found on systems run by kids in the U.S. Fridrik Skulason, a pudgy anti-virus software developer from Iceland who hated these virus exchanges, too, also found his work in circulation. And British researcher Joe Hirst's disassembled code was common.

---

6 *Op. cit.*, Fred Cohen.

The ever-talkative Buchanan was quick to point this out to anyone who would listen to him for three minutes. It was "a giant pissing contest [where] the only guy getting hurt is John Q. Public!" he shouted.

"As far as the anti-virus people go, 60 percent of the files on virus exchanges are their 'goat files,'" maintained Buchanan. "Goats" were small sacrificial host programs, usually bearing some kind of trademark from an anti-virus software developer. Developers used them because they made viruses easier to examine and handle. It was quite surprising how many such files, with identifiers from anti-virus companies like S&S International or Certus, were on bulletin boards like Buchanan's Black Axis and The Hell Pit.

Buchanan, who ran Black Axis, shouted angrily about the hypocrisy of anti-virus vendors who lobbied the media and politicians for the outlawing of systems like his when the virus files on the same bulletin boards had their origins in the labs of the same vendors.

"Now, you want to crash virus exchanges," Buchanan railed. "Well, you tell me how I got all these 'goats!'"

Alan Solomon, a British anti-virus software programmer who repeatedly phoned American hackers in efforts to get information, claimed that as a researcher he had to exchange viruses with colleagues worldwide. He would pass them on to Fridrik Skulason, for instance, who, in turn, would send them to an IBM researcher, David Chess. Once viruses were out of his hands he couldn't control them, Solomon said.[7] They could go anywhere, depending upon whom Skulason or Chess chose to send them to.

Solomon talked about having moles working the virus exchange bulletin boards. The moles would troll for new viruses and send them back to the software developers. Almost every large virus bulletin board in the U.S. was frequented by computer consultants and industry part-timers hoping to gain some kind of name for themselves in the world of anti-virus research. Some were well known, some not. There was a German named Gerhard Maier who called the Black Axis and Tim Caton's Dark Coffin bulletin board system in eastern Pennsylvania. Maier would upload viruses recov-

---

7 Author's discussions with Alan Solomon, Sept-Dec., 1992.

ered from Europe and download ones he didn't recognize, taking
them back to Germany where he would turn them over to a software
company which made a product called AVScan. He arranged to
buy the contents of Caton's BBS, but the deal was almost soured
when the sysop scorched his own collection while fooling around
with the Flip virus. Caton was able to recover enough viruses to
satisfy the German, who called regularly from Frankfurt. Maier
also called John Buchanan's Black Axis and The Hell Pit. He
eventually bought Buchanan's collection, too.

Frankfurt, coincidentally, was also the home of Project Rahab.
According to Peter Schweizer's book, "Friendly Spies," Rahab was
the code name for a German intelligence group committed to using
hackers and their methods to gather information and secrets on
whatever was of high-tech interest to the Bundesnachrichtendienst,
Germany's CIA analog. Schweizer claimed the Rahab group routinely included America in its operations during the early '90s and
hired a famous German hacker, Bernd Fix, to supply a virus for
possible military applications.[8] Fix's work was well known within
the circle of experts familiar with PC viruses. He had provided
another German, Ralf Burger, with a disassembly of the Vienna
virus and a virus of his own called Rush Hour which Burger
subsequently published in his book *Computer Viruses: A High-
Tech Disease*, later renamed as *Computer Viruses and Data Protection*. Many in the anti-virus community hated Burger because
his book devoted quite a bit of space to the grubby particulars of
data mutilation and supplied the source code to Vienna and a series
of primitive overwriting viruses—programs that destroyed their
hosts on infection. Quite naturally, the Burger and Fix programs
immediately found their way into the hands of virus programmers
and bulletin board system operators worldwide.

Burger not only had written viruses, he was also in the anti-virus business. His software was sold by Abacus in the United States
as *Virus Secure*, a product that was quietly withdrawn from the
market in 1992.

----

8   Peter Schweizer, *Friendly Spies: How America's Allies are using Economic
    Espionage to Steal our Secrets*, Atlantic Monthly Press, 1993.

Although Maier was intriguing, Caton never found out precisely what the German got in return for purchasing so many viruses.

Muskrat, another notorious double agent, would trade his viruses for new ones and take them back to McAfee Associates. Viruses and their source code flowed back and forth continuously between the virus underground and software developers around the world. Some people didn't even distinguish between anti-virus programmers and virus writers. They would trade viruses with anyone who advertised them. Silent Rage, a computer security expert who infrequently performed free-lance work characterizing large numbers of viruses for Symantec and others, was one of the latter.

In an editorial for *The Crypt Newsletter* in November of 1993, the DEA's Jim Lipshultz, one of the old advisors for David Stang's *Virus News and Reviews*, wrote:

"When it comes to disseminating viruses, anti-virus product developers are no slouches themselves. If writing a [virus] is made illegal, then most, if not all, of the anti-virus industry should be arrested for distributing viruses among themselves and to the public."[9]

Paradoxically, most virus programmers publicized their creations so thoroughly in the underground that it was clear they actually wanted anti-virus developers to have them, and the sooner the better. Viruses were a way of signaling anti-virus programmers, "See how clever I am; anything you can do I can undo. Now why don't you quit fooling around and admit it." Some had a sneaking desire to make money off viruses, too, just like the successful software developers whom they regarded as peers and competitors. If virus writers didn't publicize their work for software developers, "How else will we get credit for it?" they seemed to be asking.

This kind of motivation was a far cry from the old hacker pseudo-ethic, "Information wants to be free." It was true that contemporary hackers tended to repeat this slogan over and over in their underground manuals. But in practice, it was little more than

---

9 Jim Lipshultz, "The federal government, independent virus researchers and the First Amendment", *The Crypt Newsletter*, No. 20, November, 1993.

a convenient euphemism, eyewash that obscured the underlying bedrock of hacker belief, which was: "Your information is mine for free. But everything I can grab is secret unless you have something I want which can't be free-loaded, stolen or found somewhere else."

John Buchanan, however, had already figured out how he was going to make money from being an underground virus writer. He would sell his viruses to all takers at a price that would weed out the kids in the hacker underground. At a $100 a pop, Aristotle's virus library would even pay for course work in computer information systems management at William & Mary.

Even Bulgaria's Dark Avenger hadn't been able to pull off this trick. No one would pay for his virus programming services, even though the author of the Mutation Engine was regarded as the dean of virus programmers.

The Dark Avenger, however, wasn't American and perhaps did not grasp the U.S. grail—relentless salesmanship. And Bulgaria with its poor telecommunications and dirt-poor populace was the worst place to try and sell goods or services of any stripe—it was a non-market. John Buchanan, however, had the U.S. phone system on his side. And he knew that if you waved merchandise that was intrinsically worthless in front of enough people as though it were the crown jewels, sooner or later community perception could be twisted into thinking you actually did have something to be coveted.

"I thought, 'What now?', and the obvious smacked me between the eyes," said Buchanan. "Sell 'em! It's the way of the American entrepreneur. At first, I wasn't sure there was a market for computer viruses, but let me tell you what! I was amazed at how many people wanted these things."

Buchanan advertised his collection of viral goods on the FIDO-net, an amateur computer network which spanned the globe. It was a stroke of genius. Not only did it make him even more loathed by software developers, but it was worth cash money, too.

Colostomy Bagboy and the Silicon Vortex

On New Year's Day, 1993, Dark Angel again tried to up the ante in the virus underground with the G2 virus toolkit. Billed as the "second generation" of virus production, as far beyond the PS-MPC as that software was beyond VCL, G2 was supposed to be updated frequently with more and more efficient virus code. It flopped. Few hackers saw it as anything more than a refashioning of the PS-MPC.

And Intel had thrown a curve ball at Dark Angel. The U.S. computer chip manufacturer's 386 processor was now so cheap that virus writers, like the rest of the country, were upgrading and accepting the 80386 as the new basic home machine. PS-MPC and G2 viruses—many of them, anyway—crashed forcefully on 386's due to a small bug in Dark Angel's code which tripped over the new internal mechanics of a chip that drove the machine. The chip featured something called a look-ahead instruction cache, designed to speed execution of program code. This was bad news for the PS-MPC viruses, which depended upon self-modification in memory to function correctly. The 80386's look-ahead cache, completely unintentionally, prevented this kind of virus code from executing properly. Subsequently, it became a rule of thumb that new viruses could be empirically tested to see if they were merely PS-MPC hacks by executing them on any 80386 against a variety of host programs. If the virus in question screwed up immediately, it was probably a PS-MPC knock-off.

However, the would-be virus writers flooding into the computer underground in 1993 didn't have much technical skill. They would use one of Dark Angel's tools to make a virus and upload it as digital currency on some underground board. Few tested their creations, so they failed to notice the viruses didn't work. Anti-virus software developers called the duds "intended viruses" and shoveled them into the numbers they were reporting to consumers anyway.

Although the computer press still claimed virus programmers were clever, disgruntled computer gurus, the ugly truth was that just about anyone with a rudimentary knowledge of assembly language could write a virus. This opened the playing field to thousands of professional and hobbyist programmers and computer dabblers, from junior high school on up. Robin Raskin, a contributing editor at *PC Magazine*, expressed a typically dazed view when she spoke of "awe of the ingenuity of [virus] creators" in March, 1993.[1]

Infrequently, a virus would appear in the underground that actually was technically sweet. The EXEbug from South Africa was an example. It crammed stealth and data corruption into a mere 512 bytes, copying itself onto the hard disk and perverting the information in a machine's CMOS—an integrated circuit in which PCs retain critical system information. If someone tried to remove EXEbug from an infected computer by starting the machine clean from an uninfected disk, EXEbug's sleight-of-hand in the CMOS ensured that the infected hard disk started the system anyway, making it something of a pain for the unwitting to disinfect. This trick didn't always work, but the concept sure had the anti-virus industry talking. But EXEbug was confined to South Africa.

There were others, like Tremor, a German virus which was polymorphic and extremely stealthy. It also took some clever steps to preempt anti-virus software. It created a stir but posed no real threat to U.S. PCs. And there was Satan Bug, another polymorph written by a completely over-the-top 16-year-old San Diego *wunderkind* who went by the name of Little Loc. Little Loc wanted to

---

1   Robin Raskin with M. E. Kabay, "Antivirus software: Keeping up your guard", *PC Magazine*, March 16, 1993.

be the American version of the Dark Avenger, and Satan Bug, after it blew the Secret Service's network off-line for three days in late 1993, gave him the title hands down. However, potent viruses of this nature didn't even make up 0.1 percent of the number of strains being bandied about by software developers.

In the United States, the action in the underground migrated to a loose network of specialty BBSes which devoted themselves to accumulating the largest libraries of on-line viruses. There were systems like Hell Pit and Cryptic Morgue which carried large numbers of viruses and no doubt disturbed the equanimity of the computer conservatives who stumbled across them, but it would take the ever industrious Aristotle and his Black Axis to set the model which most would try to copy.

Aristotle, whose real name was John Buchanan, got his viruses from a colorful hacker named Guido Sanchez. Sanchez was a friend of Nowhere Man's and in addition to hanging out on Hell Pit, ran his own system in the 708 area code called Nun Beaters Anonymous, or NBA for short.

"I have nothing against nuns. Nuns are great people. I love nuns!" said Sanchez. Nun Beaters was just one of those immediately rude and catchy names fashionable in the computer underground, in this case snatched from a newspaper comic. "I regarded viruses as only good for entertainment," laughed Sanchez.

Sanchez, in his wandering throughout cyberspace, had accumulated about 300 viruses—a small number now, but a major hoard in 1992. Sanchez set up Nun Beaters so that anyone who called could have all 300 viruses in one giant download. No trade necessary. No need for leech protocols at Nun Beaters. Everyone could have the store—free!

Buchanan got his first 300 viruses—the digital seed money for Black Axis—from Nun Beaters. In Aristotelian fashion, Buchanan would go on and on about the generosity of Sanchez. Guido was a king of men, a true mensch, an ace of the underground.

"I wish he would stop that," said Sanchez.

But the damage was done. Guido's fame was nationwide in the underground. Others mimicked Nun Beaters.

Like John Buchanan, Tim Caton of the Dark Coffin BBS in eastern Pennsylvania found it easy to build up a massive virus library once he knew where to look.

Caton, who used the handle Pallbearer, also glommed onto the FIDO-net as a convenient means of advertising. The FIDO-net, Caton observed, had two electronic mail feeds devoted to spreading the warning about viruses and advertising various types of anti-virus shareware. Pallbearer showed up in one named Virus and announced he had viruses for trade at the Dark Coffin.

In a matter of days, the mail feed's moderator—a kind of straw boss in charge of enforcing etiquette and the FIDO-net's idiosyncratic concepts of political correctness—tried to ban Caton from the network. Advertising viruses, unlike advertising anti-virus software, was heretical activity and branded you cyberscum.

Caton ignored the ban, which was practically unenforceable anyway, and soon the Dark Coffin had a growing library of viruses contributed by callers from Southern California to Greenland. A Dutch virus writer calling himself Dark Helmet mailed his entire collection to Caton in return for whatever the sysop had on-line.

An assembly programmer from Southern California named Gary Watson showed up on Dark Coffin to trade viruses and source code. Watson was also vocal on the FIDO-net where he tended to side with those who considered the sysops of virus exchanges digital slime. On the FIDO-net, Watson indicated he never traded viruses with such people.

Caton promptly declared Watson a hyprocrite. He uploaded a record of Watson's exchanged viruses and source code on Dark Coffin to the FIDO-net for everyone to view. Watson retaliated by digging into Caton's private life. He broadcast Caton's age, home address and where he worked—a neighborhood McDonald's. The inference was that anyone who worked at McDonald's—even if he was a high school student trying to earn some spare change—was beneath contempt in the lofty world of the FIDO-net. It was a common tactic on the networks: rooting around for private details in the lives of your foes and posting them publicly in an electronic group mail feed which circuited the globe. Then everyone could start cackling over the personal foibles of those singled out for attack. Again and again hackers, computer nerds and professionals who were supposed to know better routinely violated the privacy of people they got into electronic tiffs with. For people who claimed to value their rights in cyberspace so highly, as a group they played fast and loose with the privacy of others.

The noise from the virus bulletin board systems in the United States was becoming so loud it began to attract virus programmers from overseas. The first one on the scene in a public manner was a British hacker who called himself Apache Warrior.

Apache Warrior had just started his own virus-programming group, called ARCV, which he said stood for the Association of Really Cruel Viruses. Since every association has an official organ, ARCV began producing an electronic journal devoted to publishing its viruses.

Modelled after *40Hex*, the ARCV magazine was short on actual virus code but long on excellent publicity. It explained ARCV's raison d'etre.

"ARCV is a organisation that is involved in Writing and Research of computer viruses," proclaimed the first issue of the ARCV News. "We hold a Library of IBM Computer viruses for the use of the ARCV members . . . We have a Bi-Monthly newsletter with the latest virus news from around the country and from around the world, virus [disassemblies] and other . . . We have links with PHALCON/SKISM in the US, we also have links with some Eastern Europe Virus writers."

While interesting, it wasn't exactly true. Hacking groups, as a rule, exaggerate the extent of their organization and links to others perceived to be more famous.

When I asked phalcon/SKISM's Dave Goldsmith about ARCV he said he wasn't familiar with their newsletter. In fact, ARCV wasn't mentioned in phalcon/SKISM's *40Hex* magazine until after Apache Warrior was arrested by Scotland Yard, months after the distribution of ARCV's first newsletter.

" . . . at the moment we are mainly English students that wish to beat and know more about the system," wrote Apache Warrior. ARCV's only other member was ICE-9, he continued, who " . . . [was] a Electronics guy who turned to the computer [sic] he writes viruses and is into Heavy Metal . . . We aim to provide the ARCV members and some Non-Members an insight to the computer underground world . . . "

Apache Warrior dutifully uploaded ARCV viruses and newsletters to Cybernetic Violence in Montreal, the home system of NuKE virus programmer Rock Steady, and John Buchanan's Black Axis. From those sites, it would take less than a day for ARCV's material to be dispersed to other systems around the country.

To ARCV, quantity was quality, and the group cranked out close to 30 viruses in only a few months in late 1992. The viruses served as advertisements for Apache Warrior, "ARCV Pres.," as he billed himself in them.

Other ARCV viruses would feature wry comments such as "McAfee— eat hot lead" and "OH NO, NOT MORE ARCV." ARCV also used Dark Angel's PS-MPC to boost production.

Alan Solomon, the developer of *Dr. Solomon's Anti-virus Toolkit*, noticed and began talking about ARCV in garrulous transatlantic phone calls to John Buchanan and myself. In the war against computer viruses, Solomon rather weirdly compared himself to Winston Churchill leading the United Kingdom against the Nazis during the darkest hours of the London Blitz. "I can promise you blood, sweat, toil and tears," wrote Solomon of himself while echoing Churchill.[2]

Solomon wanted all the information he could get on virus writers: who they were, how to get in touch with them, what people thought of their programs. He was also free with his opinions: Aristotle was the most productive virus writer, but his programs were just PS-MPC hacks. Nowhere Man was the only programmer with a shred of cleverness in NuKE, Rock Steady's viruses were the work of a nincompoop. ARCV was prolific, he laughed, but Apache Warrior's main forte was public relations. As a virus writer he and ICE-9 were busts. There was little chance their creations would spread in the wild.

The reason Solomon was so interested in virus programmers was because he believed arresting and criminally prosecuting one was a necessary precedent to halting virus production.

Solomon was fond of retelling the story of Dr. Joseph Popp, a malicious software programmer who was extradited to London in 1991 to stand trial for distributing what became known as the AIDS Information Trojan.

---

2 Alan Solomon & Tim Kay, *Dr. Solomon's PC Anti-virus Book*, New-Tech/Butterworth-Heinemann, 1994. "That's my promise to you," wrote Solomon. ". . . the blood of the anti-virus companies that fall by the wayside as the problems become more difficult, the toil of the virus researchers . . . the cold sweat of the users as they realize that they have a virus . . . and the tears that will be shed when it is realised that a virus has not merely erasEd all data . . . but that it is no longer possible to tell which backups are valid . . . 'We shall never surrender.'"

Popp was an erratic scientist living in Cleveland, Ohio, in 1989 who had concocted a wild scheme to extort money from computer users in Europe. Popp had programmed a software booby-trap that masqueraded as a database containing information on AIDS and how to assess an individual's risk of contracting the disease. The database, as one might expect, was trivial and contained only the barest information about the disease. However, when an unwitting user installed the software, the AIDS Information Trojan created hidden directories and files on the computer while hiding a counter in one of the system's start-up files, the AUTOEXEC.BAT. Once the count reached 90, Popp's creation would encrypt all the files on the machine and present the operator with a message to send approximately $200 to a post office box in Panama City for a cure reversing the effects of his program. The AIDS Information Trojan came with a vaguely menacing warning not to install the software if one didn't fully intend to pay for it at once.

Popp mailed 20,000 diskettes to users in Europe, apparently mostly subscribers to a failed magazine called *PC Business World*. His plan began to come apart when the U.S. invaded Panama on the day his diskettes began to arrive in England. The ill nature of Popp's database was quickly uncovered. It's unknown if anyone actually paid Popp for his software bomb, but the subscription list of *PC Business World* was examined and Popp identified as the AIDS Information Cyborg's author. New Scotland Yard then drew up papers to have him extradited on blackmail charges, a process that took almost another two years.

With Popp finally in England, the case flopped. Lawyers claimed he was unfit to stand trial because he began wearing a cardboard box over his head. The prosecution was stymied. It was impossible to determine if Popp was indeed *non compos mentis* or merely shamming. So authorities ejected him from the country. Solomon felt that the Popp case was a good example of how to go after malicious programmers, not the embarrassing boondoggle others saw it as. He thought it showed English authorities were flush with success and completely prepared to extradite manufacturers of dangerous code, including virus writers, for trial from anywhere in the West.[3]

In a perfect world, Solomon thought, ARCV could be the next example to strike fear in the hearts of digital fiends like virus writers. Once rounded up for writing and distributing their viruses, its members could be arm-twisted into ratting out their compatriots in the United States, who would then also be turned over to New Scotland Yard to await trial.

This was called "turning Queen's evidence," said Solomon.

It was extreme bad luck for Apache Warrior when he was arrested for a crime completely unrelated to virus writing in December of 1992. Apache Warrior, said Solomon, was bagged when police from Manchester arrested him and seized his computer following a complaint that he had been stealing phone service from British Telecom. The virus programmer had been running a line from his telephone to a neighbor's with the result that the neighbor was billed for all the ARCV president's long distance calls. The police merely followed the line back to its point of origin and arrested Apache Warrior at the other end, said Solomon.

At this point, said Solomon, someone noticed Apache Warrior's computer had quite a few viruses stored on it and decided to contact New Scotland Yard's computer crime unit.

Solomon was called in as a technical advisor on the case and was able to convince New Scotland Yard's computer crime unit that it should also try to prosecute Apache Warrior as a virus writer. The rest of the group could be rounded up for good measure, too. Solomon claimed that even though prosecuting hackers for virus writing was hard, it was always easy to get them on the basis of other material stored on their PCs such as stolen credit information, ill-gotten passwords to proprietary systems and such. New Scotland Yard then went forward with local constabularies and conducted raids at multiple sites in England in January, 1993, arresting another man, ARCV member ICE-9, in the sweep, which was code-named Apache.

At the time, there were no reported incidences of ARCV viruses on the computers of the citizenry. *Virus News International*, by extension S&S International—Solomon's company organ—solicited readers for any evidence concerning ARCV viruses in unwelcome places but the effort was fruitless. ARCV's viruses, while famous in anti-virus circles, were pathetic as public threats.

---

3 Note: Popp's AIDS trojan was *not* a virus. —*ed.*

In the meantime, Apache Warrior settled with British Telecom on the fraud charge and the case against the English virus writers began to stall.

Solomon was still jawboning John Buchanan, however.

He told the American virus writer he had been implicated as a member of ARCV—he was not—and that Scotland Yard might be interested in extraditing him for trial for aiding in distributing ARCV viruses. Buchanan became frantic. He only knew what Solomon had chosen to tell him about Joseph Popp, that the AIDS Information Trojan programmer had been extradited from Cleveland to London with the cooperation of the FBI. Buchanan didn't know that the case had fallen apart with no conviction. It seemed reasonable to him that he might soon be heading to England in shackles on the mere say-so of Solomon and a member of ARCV whom he barely knew as a member of Black Axis's circle of overseas callers.

While Apache Warrior talked big about ARCV's presence in the world of virus writing, the group never had any links that would make for convincing court testimony about international conspiracy. Worse, its viruses weren't destroying anyone's data. And as Alan Solomon continued to broadcast the arrests and the nature of the evidence against ARCV on the Internet, the case completely unraveled. In the end, the ARCV arrests were even less significant than the story of Joseph Popp, although it was the end of the road for Apache Warrior's virus writing. English computer crime police, with the prodding of Alan Solomon, had once again attempted to punish the wicked—in this case the bumptious but feeble hackers of ARCV—and fumbled, ultimately because the presumed culprits weren't as convincing boogeymen as portrayed by their own electronic press releases.

In the virus underground, it was business as usual. Hardly anyone missed ARCV. However one virus writer— Little Loc, the author of Satan Bug and a series of increasingly more nasty and sophisticated fast infectors—wrote a virus called Payback which would swat the data every January 27 on a PC's hard disk in symbolic retaliation for the fate that had befallen ARCV. Little Loc had disguised Payback in a copy of a piece of software used by McAfee Associates called VALIDATE. People who used McAfee's software frequently used VALIDATE to check the integrity of his programs. If they wound up with a copy of Little Loc's

VALIDATE however, the only thing that was going to happen was that their hard disk would be "validated" with a copy of Payback. Exactly who, though, was to be paid back for Apache Warrior's arrest the virus didn't make clear.

Little Loc uploaded Payback and other viruses to Caustic Contagion, a system run by Brian Oblivion, the same hacker who had been excommunicated from NuKE's neck of cyberspace for arguing with Rock Steady about the stupidity of making the the GenVir virus toolkit appear as if it had been infected by a virus. Caustic Contagion, operated out of a bedroom in Waco, Texas, was one in a growing number of bulletin board systems which stocked Hell Pit-size volumes of viruses and sent e-mail to each other on a semi-private world-spanning network operating as a shadow of the FIDO-net. Sometimes billed as VxNet, sometimes as NuKEnet, sometimes as both, the virus exchange links exchanged gossip and allowed various virus programmers to chat or engage in vitupera-tive, unproductive arguments with each other.

Little Loc enjoyed Caustic Contagion. Oblivion and Little Loc had gotten to know each other on Prodigy, the family-oriented on-line service run by Sears and IBM. Oblivion was avuncular, and knowledgeable about viruses. There were also a few Caustic Con-tagion callers who would, from time to time, compliment Little Loc on Satan Bug or some other virus he had written. While in resi-dence, Little Loc changed his handle to Priest and began associating himself with phalcon/SKISM, although the actual collaboration between the hacker and the other members of the virus-program-ming group was minimal.

The nascent virus exchange network, of which Caustic Conta-gion was a part, included Black Axis, Cybernetic Violence in Montreal, Tim Caton's Dark Coffin and a handful of systems in Europe, Australia and South Africa. Almost by default—since no one was really in charge of the network—Buchanan's Black Axis dominated.

Sara Gordon was an observer on the network and wrote a series of articles for *Virus News International*.[4] It was her premise that the American virus exchanges could trace their origins back to a

---

4 *Op. cit.*, Gordon.

system run in Sofia, Bulgaria, by a student called Todor Todorov. The Sofia virus exchange, according to Gordon, was the original— everyone else was a copycat. It was the home of the Dark Avenger, too—the virus programmer who had written the Mutation Engine and dedicated the first MtE virus to her.

The American virus exchange network, claimed Gordon, was set up to rapidly transfer technical information and viruses between systems to wherever a struggling virus author needed a push or timely advice on how to engage in computer sabotage. The virus exchanges were fomenting digital mistrust and their existence was an affront to respectable telecommunications enthusiasts. They "endangered the future of computing," wrote Gordon, and put "information systems under attack."

It was good copy but loaded with a kind of exaggeration that was a *pro forma* requirement for writing in a mainstream computer publication or industry advertiser.

None of the systems operators vocal in the network were familiar firsthand with Todor Todorov's virus exchange in Sofia, Bulgaria. If they had heard of it, it was usually through some piece of anti-virus software propaganda which found its way into plagiarized electronic documents or magazine copy.

Much of the real bandwidth in electronic mail among these systems was devoted to petty turf wars and savage, obscenity-laced public quarrels over who was bigger, badder, smarter or the boss. Buchanan, by now a member of NuKE, was already arguing with other hackers in the group. Sara Gordon was also a favored scapegoat. Eventually this resulted in the pornographic NewSara virus already mentioned.

However, the actual technical information on viruses being passed back and forth was nil. If a master plan was being hatched to subvert the future of computing, it was fiendishly clever, because it was totally invisible.

The sale of viruses was real, though. While Tim Caton's high school computer teacher was lecturing classes about the "impossibility" of data communications by modem at speeds greater than 2400 baud, the eastern Pennsylvania virus exchange sysop was connecting with overseas callers at 14000 baud and shipping the viruses he had off to the strangest places.

One purchaser was a caller from Edegedesminde, Greenland, who travelled cyberspace under the whimsical handle of Santa.

Santa claimed to be working in telephone security in Greenland but there was no way of knowing for sure. Still, Caton would smile to himself wondering about the uses of viruses in cold, remote Greenland. Another shipment of viruses went to a Navy man stationed on the USS San Francisco out of Pearl Harbor. Buchanan continued to peddle his viruses, too. One client was an Austrian from Vienna by the name of Franz Swoboda. Swoboda was a colorful fellow in virus history. In 1987 Swoboda discovered what he called the Charlie virus. Ralf Burger recovered a copy of Charlie from Swoboda and passed it on to his colleague Bernd Fix. Fix, whom you remember was tabbed by Germany's Bundesnachrichtendienst to write virus code for military applications, analyzed Swoboda's Charlie virus and submitted the work to Burger, who published it in his book *Computer Viruses and Data Protection*. It became the Vienna virus and was widely copied by virus writers everywhere.

Swoboda lived near Vienna and he wanted to join the Computer Anti-virus Research Organization (CARO), a predominantly Euro-American self-appointed pan-professional group of programmers in the software and virus research business. Alan Solomon was one of CARO's founding members, as were Fridrik Skulason and Vesselin Bontchev, an expatriate Bulgarian computer science graduate student.

CARO wanted no part of Swoboda and enlisted one of its American members, Glenn Jordan of Datawatch Corporation, to ask John Buchanan for information on the Austrian. The idea was that if Buchanan would fink on Swoboda, telling CARO that the Austrian had purchased viruses from him, it would be easy for the group to dismiss the discoverer of the Charlie virus as a troublemaker who collaborated with virus writers. Underneath the intrigue was the implication that Swoboda might actually be the author of the original Charlie/Vienna virus.

Buchanan hemmed and hawed and told me about it, but said he declined to give Jordan the desired information. Swoboda never made it into CARO, though.

The virus sales were good business for Buchanan. They netted him thousands of dollars and lots of needed computer equipment. He even sold one of the NuKE hacking group's unpublished virus tools, the NED, or NuKE Encryption Device.

The NED had been written by Nowhere Man and was meant to supplant the Dark Avenger's Mutation Engine as an advanced piece of code used to disguise new viruses. Nowhere Man had spent some time on it and to him, it was a far more satisfying project than the Virus Creation Laboratory. He transferred a copy of the NED to another NuKE programmer, Rock Steady, who in turn forwarded it to Buchanan. Buchanan promptly sold the NED along with the rest of his viruses, even though it wasn't supposed to be formally passed around in the underground. He also sent a copy of his collection to Alan Solomon, with whom he continued to have a schizophrenic on-again-off-again love-hate relationship.

The NED was a tool that wasn't included in viruses anywhere at the time it was sold, but it effectively demonstrated the downright twisted involuntary combination stranglehold and symbiosis anti-virus software developers and virus writers were locked in during 1992-93.

The first and only virus using Nowhere Man's NED was called ITSHARD and was, quite oddly, not written by the VCL author. ITSHARD came from Europe, straight from the corrupt thicket of fringe anti-virus researchers and mysterious Germans who made up John Buchanan's virus sales list. Buchanan had sold the NED, along with his entire virus collection to Gerhard Maier. But the copy of the NED which Nowhere Man had released to Rock Steady was unfinished. It had a minor bug which rendered it non-functional after a few turns of the code. It needed to be corrected. Maier, in turn, indicated to Buchanan he had tinkered with the NED, with the aim of fixing the code's instability, and then turned it over to a Dutch anti-virus researcher named Righard Zwienenberg. Zwienenberg wanted to produce one of the first pieces of anti-virus software to detect NED viruses. The only problem was, there were no NED viruses. This was only a trifling obstacle. Suddenly, Zwienenberg had a copy of a new virus—wink-wink—called IT-SHARD which was the only such program which actually used the NED. He gave Maier a copy. Maier promptly couriered it right back to Buchanan.

Buchanan's copy of ITSHARD eventually criss-crossed the Atlantic once again, this time into the hands of Alan Solomon. ITSHARD combined Nowhere Man's encryption code with Dark Angel's p/S-MPC virus code. The NED blew Solomon away, invalidating much of the work he had put into his own anti-virus software.

"... it does everything in a hundred different ways; it uses word and byte registers, there are lots of noisy nonsense bytes, little jumps ... The NED looked like something out of a Salvador Dali nightmare and I thought it was going to take a month of programming [to detect ITSHARD]," he wrote in his 1994 book on PC viruses.[5]

Solomon threw up his hands in despair and decided to go back to a project he called the Ugly Duckling which had gone up a blind alley and been shelved. He thought it might have some application in helping to unravel the thorny problem of NED detection. The result was a major revision of his software, the fruition of proprietary programming techniques called the Virtran language used in it, and a Queen's Award for Technological Achievement in 1993. The single NED virus—ITSHARD—still isn't in the wild almost two years after Nowhere Man wrote the original encryption code.

Nowhere Man never put the first copy of the NED into any viruses. After hearing that Buchanan had sent it to everyone in creation and even charged some people for it, he corrected the bug, tested the code against Righard Zwienenberg's anti-NED detector—which no longer worked against his program—and buried it. "The NED is the one thing I'm most proud of," said Nowhere Man.

For Buchanan, it was time to stir the pot again. He renamed Black Axis the Virginia Institute of Virus Research, closed it to some but not all of its callers, and asked Alan Solomon to let him into CARO.

Solomon attended a conference of computer security experts in March 1993 in New York City, where he met with some of the other American representatives of CARO. Buchanan's name was put before the others at the meeting, along with Sara Gordon's and that of a former Solomon employee, Iolo Davidson. This was supposed to be secret business but a hacker from phalcon/SKISM named TimeLord had also been asked to attend the security conference. TimeLord was bored so he decided to do what hackers

5 *Op. cit.*, Solomon & Kay.

sometimes do in their spare time: go rifling through the trash of others.

He recovered the schedule of events Solomon had outlined for the informal CARO meeting at the conference. In the days that followed, he turned it over to Buchanan and anyone else in the virus underground who was interested in seeing it.

In addition to putting Buchanan's name before CARO members in attendance as a would-be nominee, the schedule showed Solomon wanted to seal the leak allowing the flow of viruses from software developers into the computer underground. To this end, the CARO virus collection would have to be uniquely marked, so that copies of viruses could be traced from hand to hand. It was also necessary to deny there even was an official CARO virus collection. "I think that it is really important that there be no such thing. That way, if people ask for it, or claim they have it, then it's nonsense," wrote Solomon.

There would also have to be action taken against virus writing groups. ARCV was gone, but now it was an American problem. Some American members of CARO—Joe Wells of Symantec, maker of the Norton Anti-Virus, Glenn Jordan of Datawatch and another—could be given the job if they wanted it. It was time to set up a secret database of virus writers containing "Handles, BBSes, Names, [and] Addresses," according to the memo. The objective would be to get a police prosecution against anyone who was committing a crime "but not, of course, against anyone who is not committing a crime."

In the meantime, Buchanan was trying to convince other systems connected to the virus exchange network to set up their own franchises using the generic naming convention "The [Put Your Locale Here] Institute of Virus Research." There was the Oklahoma Institute of Virus Research in Oklahoma City. Its sysop, Paskell "Geno" Paris, eventually wound up in jail after a tortuous and ugly series of events we'll hear of later. Tim Caton was ready to switch Dark Coffin to The Pennsylvania Institute of Virus Research but hesitated on the decision when Nowhere Man called him a sheep for doing the bidding of Buchanan. Dark Coffin's name change was put on hold permanently when Gerhard Maier attempted to buy Caton's viruses and the sysop was forced to scramble to recover them after disastrously allowing the Flip virus to run loose on his computer. By the time the mess was cleaned up, Caton had received an offer to serve as a congressional intern in Washington, D.C., over the summer. He took down Dark Coffin and departed from the world of virus exchanges. In Cicero, Illinois, a large virus system known as The Vine changed its name to the Greater Chicago Institute of Virus Research. Much later it would be switched again, this time to the Computer Virus Research and Information Service.

Buchanan's idea was to make an end run around the anti-virus software developers plying the networks. The Institutes of Virus Research would advertise themselves as information providers on viruses and claim commercial independence from the software peddlers. It was a fevered dream in which, ideally, the institute managers would collect viruses from the authors and send them on to anti-virus software developers as well as other interested parties. To those on the outside looking in, not much had changed, however.

The sysop of the Black Axis/Virginia Institute of Virus Research went forward with plans to place another message feed on the FIDO-net called NuKE_theWorld, with himself as moderator. This would bring the wisdom of the NuKE virus programmers to the FIDO-net audience en masse. The message feed picked up some steam and appeared on its way into the FIDO-net mainstream when Buchanan abruptly lost interest and closed the Black Axis for a short period of time surrounding his landing a job in mid-1993 with a military contractor in the Newport News area. When this happened, the NuKE members on Cybernetic Violence took over and continued to try and extend what had become known as the NuKE-net. It was all very tangled.

Adding to the confusion was the self-styled cyber-terrorist, Paskell "Geno" Paris. Paris, a nurse by day, ran a bulletin board system in Oklahoma City which flip-flopped between the names Vortex and The Oklahoma Institute of Virus Research. It was part of John Buchanan's network of systems which had become inextricably mixed-up with the FIDO-net bulletin boards devoted to spreading advertising for shareware anti-virus software, much to the annoyance of the software developers and their representatives.

When not in the mainstream mail areas of the FIDO-net, Paris would call other systems under aliases like Colostomy Bagboy and others too perverse to print. He published a profane, hideously violent electronic magazine known as Vortex. Vortex was an oil stain covering the windshield to those used to driving slowly down the center lane of the information highway, or what there was of it on the FIDO-net. Vortex was also hysterically funny.

If you didn't know what you were doing, reading Vortex was also kind of like walking through a minefield. Colostomy Bagboy included tips and advice for playing with viruses, which, if followed, would result in the inexperienced corrupting the data on their computers. In Vortex, the editor explained his world view. The networks were a silicon vortex, Colostomy Bagboy proclaimed. His philosophy was a metaphysical pseudo-serious gobble which combined junk pop culture, received wisdom and an assortment of fictions flogged by the likes of William Gibson, "Dune's" Frank Herbert, Anne Rice and Steven Donaldson.

"The VORTEX is this and more . . . ," wrote Paris. "[In] this medium there is only continued flux, the pursuit of information, and joyful destruction. Steven Donaldson's Despiser is our only god and anarchy is our only goal."

The Despiser, or Lord Foul, was the arch villain in Donaldson's Illearth War series of books, a sort of cheap rip-off of J. R. R. Tolkien's "Lord of The Rings." Paul Mua'Dib, the hero of the book "Dune," also tended to get invoked as spiritual shaman in Colostomy Bagboy's Vortex.

However, Paris was no cyberpunk, he said. He hated the word.

"Cyberpunk is the term that [William] Gibson gave that highly technical group of phreakers\hackers in his hi-tech fictional world," he wrote in Vortex.

"Man, a punk is somebody who bends over and takes it up the ass. . . Personally, I have always liked the term that Vesselin Bontchev—a much over-rated virus researcher—gave the Dark Avenger. In one of his extremely boorish papers he called DA a 'Technopath'. . . Thanks Vesselin . . .

"There are many ways to obtain godhood in The SILICON VORTEX, however, if you can leave the false worldly constrains of ethics and morals behind . . . Creation is always nice, but true power rests in the power to destroy.

"The information contained within [Vortex] . . . will give you the ability to tap into that dark side of yourself that likes to cause anarchy. When you cross the line, your desire to create the anarchy of destruction will become almost all consuming . . . True gratification comes in the creative and stylish destruction of other's data based inside the VORTEX."

For those unfamiliar with the argot of the computer underground, the words of Colostomy Bagboy were enough to set hair ablaze. However, within the underground it fit a mold of standard, if cleverly written, rabble-rousing malevolence exceeding the documentation and function of Nowhere Man's Virus Creation Laboratory only by degrees. In other words, it fit the lay of the land. The FIDO-net, or Paris's silicon vortex, was ripe for a kind of low-level hacking version of search and destroy. FIDO-net was sustained by a diverse collection of hobbyists and computer professionals who spent quite a deal of their spare time building up its electronic mail capabilities which encompassed sending astronomical volumes of database-like messaging from system to system in a mind-numbingly complicated web which stretched around the planet. Because it was cobbled together from countless different and poorly understood, poorly documented, poorly supported software mixtures, the FIDO-net was a security nightmare riddled with gaping loopholes which could be exploited to sow fear and insane hatred among its managers. While pernicious hacking on the FIDO-net may have seemed like a neat trick, it was the equivalent of pulling wings off flies.

One of Paris's favorite technopathic tricks was the manipulation and fabrication of mail within the structure of the FIDO-net. He would select a well-read electronic message feed and concoct an elaborate series of irritating, tasteless and sophomoric messages packed with puzzling lies, spittle-spraying-from-the-mouth diatribes and sexual language of the vilest sort.

In his own words:

```
Single message bases are called echos, and are
organized by a moderator. All posts are ex-
pected to deal with the particular subject of
the echo. Example: Posts in the abortion echo
are expected to concern abortion, posts in the
Holy_Bible echo are expected to deal with the
Bible. Moderators who do not understand the in-
herent nature of the VORTEX become quite peeved
when one gets off subject. They get all pissed
and become unhappy Babylonians.
```

Paris published the Aristo-Hack, John Buchanan's program which manufactured 500 PS-MPC viruses, in Vortex, along with software to automate the production of fabricated mail chains of purely inflammatory quality. He would brag of launching these electronic mail stink bombs into the network from time to time. He was also snatching the regular message bases devoted to virus information on the net and transferring them to the NuKE_THEWORLD systems. This created a continuous war between the moderators of the virus information feeds, who were only interested in pushing various shareware anti-virus software kits, and the virus writers on NuKE_THEWORLD who wanted only to sell viruses (like Buchanan), point out the shortcomings of anti-virus software and bait the shareware peddlers.

One of the moderators of the virus information echos was a European by the name of Edwin Cleton. Cleton was constantly threatening anyone who didn't agree with him with banishment from the FIDO-net echo he controlled.

He would, he said, "Hit them with his electronic baseball bat." These were brainless, empty threats in cyberspace but Cleton's pompous and doctrinaire manner made him an immediate target for the virus programmers, including Paris.

The security of Cleton's FIDO echo was abominable in America, and Paris, doing what he liked best, manipulated the mail and staging within the network so that Cleton, through confusion and inattention, was cut off from control of his own turf. Paris had literally hijacked the mail, proclaiming himself the new moderator and Edwin Cleton an unwanted pest. The anarchy so beloved by Colostomy Bagboy reigned.

"Edwin is so pissed off," laughed Paris at one point. Cleton was indeed incensed. He accused Paris of being a child pornographer, a claim that made the mad hacker chuckle.

Even Paris's friends were buffaloed. Terminator, an acquaintance from Missouri, who collaborated with Paris in the fabrication and deployment of mail bombs into the FIDO-net Midwest architecture, confessed Colostomy Bagboy was a wild man, prone to crazy fabrications.

"You just never know with Geno," he said. "Geno talks and talks and after a while, anything could be true."

Paris got heavily into phreaking telephone calls, said Terminator. Terminator thought Colostomy Bagboy was into the whole evil hacker scofflaw trip, trying to get free phone service and messing with credit card information. The Missouri hacker became disinterested.

Then Colostomy Bagboy walked over even his line by, according to Paris, messing with the Federal Bureau of Investigation's National Crime Information Center computer. Paris claimed to have invaded the NCIC system, a computer network which contains the national criminal activity database used by lawmen across the country. NCIC is raw criminal data which can tell a cop taking a hit-and-run driver in for booking in California whether the suspect is wanted on different charges in other states. The FBI takes NCIC rather seriously and when Colostomy Bagboy attempted to upload one of his logic bombs into it, a storm of trouble crashed down on him, he said.

Minutes after he had connected via modem with NCIC and hung up, someone had called him back and said merely, "Gotcha" over the phone. The FBI scooped him up and in the days that followed, agents proceeded to grill him about details on the virus underground, Paris said. Who was Rock Steady? What did Paris know about John Buchanan and myself, the editor of *The Crypt Newsletter*? What did a virus writer named Memory Lapse, Nowhere Man and the rest have to do with the alleged virus infection of the President and Hillary's Health Care Plan information diskettes earlier in the year?

Back in the real world, it was quite a different story. Paris was indicted by a federal grand jury and jailed in late 1993 on the far more prosaic felony charges of forgery, making false claims, possession of a stolen credit card (later dismissed), possession of photo license of another, and related counts. He pleaded guilty, was convicted and sentenced to serve a twelve-month stint in prison, administered by the state of Oklahoma and the federal government. Paskell Paris, according to federal indictment CR-93-255R, "falsely represented himself to be Michael Glen Paris" and had engaged in activities aimed at hijacking the identity of someone named Michael Paris for his own uses.

Weirdly, Paskell Paris's friends in cyberspace had no idea what really had happened to him, just that he was in jail. Terminator knew Colostomy Bagboy was up the river for at least a year and that was it. Finally, he received mail from Paris in the Oklahoma City jail which declared, in typical Bagboy megalomaniacal style:

For those that did not know, I am in here suf-
fering and paying penance for your sins.

The United States of America, supposed land of
the free imprisons more people than any other
nation on the face of the earth.[6]

The "information highway" is a joke. This was
proven when they arrested me for supposed "hacking" on the NCIC. We have no freedom of expression or speech . . . Rise up, oh sons and
daughters, in bloody revolution against the op-
pressive regime! Like Nelson Mandela before me
I will suffer.

While Paris was far from the information highway's anti-Christ,
his Vortex persona had spun a legend that convinced his targets and
peers he was one bad dude. It was the end of the Oklahoma Institute
of Virus Research.

---

6 Unfortunately quite true.—*ed.*

Some Finks Pick on a Lady

Fame—or infamy—within the computer underground often comes from the strangest quarters. Few card-carrying "Question authority!" sloganeers would have guessed that in 1993, one of the biggest stories would be the scandal surrounding security expert Kim Clancy and her U.S. Department of the Treasury Security Branch bulletin board system.

An ex-Arizonan and graduate of DeVry Institute of Technology, that electronics and telecommunications training school dunned into the consciousness of every TV-watching American, Clancy came to the world of computer systems and network security after a career in the military. There she was part of a team whose job it was to handle "Broken Arrows," mishaps in which nuclear bombs are either lost, broken, burned or otherwise mangled and mishandled.

Clancy eventually came to work for the Treasury Department, in the Bureau of the Public Debt's Office of Automated Information Systems. While she was there, Clancy's department—Security Branch— began running a bulletin board system for its employees out of the departmental office in Parkersburg, West Virginia.

In 1991, when the system was first put on-line, it served as a private clearinghouse for boilerplate policy documents, articles from the department's internal security newsletter and bulletins issued by the Computer Emergency Response Team—the organization put together after Cornell student Robert Morris's worm program struck Internet-linked mainframe computers nationwide.

Gradually, said Clancy, the system was opened to the public, mostly as a courtesy and convenience to other government and private sector employees who had either contributed material or benefited from its database.

Then things got interesting. On the lookout for any information that would simplify her job as an administrator responsible for maintaining the security of departmental networks, Clancy began collecting copies of the famous underground hacking newsletter, *Phrack*. *Phrack* was packed with controversial and dodgy material, much of it written by hackers intimately familiar with telephonic manipulation and on-line systems intrusion. *Phrack* was so inflammatory in some circles, it was safe to say people had actually been jailed over it through the years of its publication.

One *Phrack* article on network security, written by a hacker calling himself The Butler, caught Clancy's attention. She put the issue containing it on-line on the AIS system. Much to her amazement, The Butler rang up the BBS. Intrigued, Clancy asked The Butler if he would be interested in passing on some of the software tools used in network hacking mentioned in the original *Phrack* story. The Butler was happy to oblige and Clancy subsequently put them on-line at AIS. And so hacker tools—software from the computer underground—arrived on an open U.S. government bulletin board.

Often, Clancy would say, "The Butler told me everything I know about network hacking."

Clancy began consulting with hackers and gathering their tutorials and software for display on the AIS system. This meant calling hacker bulletin boards. Eventually, she found herself in places like The Hell Pit, Guido Sanchez's Nun Beaters Anonymous and phalcon/SKISM's home-base, The Landfill. If *Phrack* could be on-line, so could *40 Hex*.

In fact, according to Clancy, it was fortunate Security Branch knew hackers like Guido Sanchez because they often proved more competent than the vendors the department called in to supply various security services. Such was the case when Security Branch entered a contract with a company from Beltsville, Maryland, called Commcrypt. Commcrypt was hired to supply site-licenses to cover installation of its anti-virus software on the Security Branch networks. Late in October of 1992 company representatives showed up in Parkersburg to install the protection. It turned out to be a very bad day. The Maltese Amoeba virus joined the party, according to Clancy.

This was serious trouble.

Maltese Amoeba spread quickly at Security Branch. It had the ability to successfully infect most types of programs and used a handful of different encryption/decryption methods to hide itself in infected files. Worse, the virus had an activation on November 1, at which time it would begin trashing hard disks while displaying part of a poem from William Blake's *Auguries of Innocence*:

> To see a world in a grain of sand
> And heaven in a wild flower,
> Hold infinity in the palm of your hand
> And eternity in a hour.
>   The Virus 16/3/91

Clancy wasn't satisfied with Commcrypt's handling of Maltese Amoeba so she put in a call to Guido Sanchez. Sanchez had a copy of the virus and his own network on which to test it. He infected the system, examined the virus's behavior and helped guide Clancy through the process of removing it from Security Branch's networks. The virus infection and clean-up resulted in the department's networks being off-line for three days.

In the meantime, Commcrypt representatives had leaked information on the incident was leaked to the publication *Federal Communications Week*. Clancy believed Commcrypt's representatives were responsible and she was furious. It was ironic that the best professional help in removing the virus had come from a sysop of the Nun Beaters Anonymous virus exchange while the Beltsville suits from Commcrypt had apparently taken the opportunity to drum up publicity for themselves in a trade publication. This cost Commcrypt, said Clancy. The company's contract was radically cut back when renewal time rolled around.

While acquaintance with the computer underground had been of real practical benefit to Clancy, and by extension Security Branch, the accumulation of issues of *40 Hex* and other examples of virus source code, including Nowhere Man's Virus Creation Laboratory, began to set off grumbling in the world of straight computer security providers. These types didn't mind having access to the material, said Clancy, but they'd be damned if anyone else could just take a look at it.

Members of CARO had been sniffing around AIS, among them Joe Wells of Symantec, who according to Clancy, had encouraged her to continue what she was doing with Security Branch. About the same time, he tried to recruit her into another pet project of the big anti-virus software developers: the maintenance of a "hush list" of bulletin board systems and suspected operators of them involved in the trade of computer viruses.

It was the shopworn Computer Antivirus Research Organization idea: Find virus exchange bulletin board systems with the aim of shutting them down, by whatever means possible. The only thing wrong with the plan, according to Clancy, was that some of the systems and organizations named on the list had no connection to the computer underground or BBSes which traded in computer viruses. Clancy declined to have anything to do with the list, viewing it as stupid and liable to result in legal retaliation.

About the same time, CARO member Klaus Brunnstein of The University of Hamburg's Virus Test Center threatened Clancy with a negative press campaign if virus source code was not removed from the AIS BBS. This nettled Clancy, who knew that other CARO associates were helping themselves to the files in contention on the system.

What occurred in the subsequent months was, for Clancy, a publicly damaging exercise which resulted when a few CARO software developers and their point men slithered out of the underbrush in the name of the community good.

Obviously, Clancy's distribution of hacker files and virus code was a controversial idea. As such, it did not sit well with this old-boy network of security professionals and anti-virus researchers and software developers of which Klaus Brunnstein was a part. Brunnstein, you recall, was the same anti-virus expert credited with floating the wildly exaggerated claims on Michelangelo infection for the Reuters news service. It was a claim he would later deny making in a 1994 book on anti-virus techniques written by another software developer, Pam Kane.[1]

---

1 Pamela Kane, *PC Security and Virus Protection Handbook*, M&T Books, 1994.

In March of 1993, Alan Solomon was into the act, hectoring a captive audience on the impropriety of virus source code on AIS at an Institute of Electrical and Electronics Engineers (IEEE) meeting of security professionals in New York City. This was the same meeting where the phalcon/SKISM hacker named TimeLord had filched Solomon's CARO memo.

Also disturbed was Ken van Wyk, the moderator of comp.virus, a weekly electronic mail collection distributed throughout the Internet and dominated by the technical babble, gossip and apocrypha of CARO members like Vesselin Bontchev and anti-virus software developer Fridrik Skulason, among others.

None of this, thought Clancy, made any difference. After all, the ramblings of electronic mail digests—rantings in the vast electronic ether of cyberspace—- are generally not taken seriously by the great majority of computer users who read them; they are just part of the background radiation that everyone is used to. Van Wyk's concern, she said, was just more of the same: inaccurate and technically silly complaints which had dogged the BBS intermittently since its inception.

Eventually, however, the concerted gossiping and background politicking was enough to break the system. The crystallizing event was one anonymous letter, published in May 1993 in *RISKS*, another Internet/Usenet electronic mail forum. Written by "anonymous," it accused the AIS BBS of distributing material that was illegal and unethical.

"This text was forwarded to me by a friend and professional colleague in the UK," "anonymous" wrote. "I am dismayed that this type of activity is being condoned by an American Governmental Agency [sic]. I can only hope that this operation is shut down and the responsible parties are reprimanded. I am extremely disturbed by the thought that my tax money is being used for, what I consider, unethical, immoral and possibly illegal activities."

Accompanying the *RISKS* post was a log of the virus source code stocked on AIS.

"Anonymous" was actually a cat's-paw of Alan Solomon. As it turned out, he was about as far from being a whistleblower, which is what the *Washington Post* dubbed him on June 19 when the AIS story broke nationwide,[2] as one could get. "Anonymous" was Paul Ferguson, an obscure security consultant and "network integrator" from Centreville, Virginia, whose main claim to fame was that he was a moderator of one of the FIDO-net virus information electronic mail feeds set up to cater to anti-virus shareware peddlers. Like Edwin Cleton, who inherited trouble by baiting virus programmers like Geno Paris, Ferguson was rigid and full of himself, used to insulting or squelching anyone in his neck of the FIDO-net not deemed politically correct.

In the months that followed, the ethics of the campaign against AIS were assailed in *Computer underground Digest*, a weekly electronic magazine distributed around the Internet dedicated to covering anything and everything under the sun addressing the sociology, criminology, and ongoing development of cyberspace.

CuD editor Jim Thomas, writing in issue 5.51, called Ferguson's *RISKS* posting "cryptic posturing." Ferguson was a user on Clancy's system, and "his feigned ignorance about aspects of the BBS, the professed fear of 'retaliation,' and the vengeful (and anonymous) call for punitive sanctions against the sysop seem more in line with an intentionally planned assault than with an ethical attempt to raise issues and generate debate," continued Thomas.

Ferguson was hardly a stranger to underground virus exchange bulletin board systems, either. He would occasionally access them to gather virus tools. John Buchanan remembered Ferguson calling him for virus code. "He wanted the Trident Polymorphic Engine because he couldn't find it anywhere else. He pleaded for it, so I gave it to him," said Buchanan.

This was contorted, hypocritical behavior from a man secretly lobbying, along with CARO members Klaus Brunnstein, Alan Solomon and Fridrik Skulason, for the removal of the AIS BBS's virus code library—- a library much less complete than Buchanan's Black Axis but much more accessible to relatively straightforward security workers hesitant to dive into the deep, uncharted pools of source code and live viruses found on many underground systems. Also lost in the hysteria was the obscure fact that CARO members had already helped themselves to virus source code on AIS. Sku-

---

2 Joel Garreau, "Treasury exposed computer virus info; whistleblowers halted display available to anyone with a modem", *The Washington Post*, June 19, 1993

lason told Clancy none of his colleagues used AIS. Clancy insisted otherwise and provided names.

However, at the end of May 1993, weeks after Ferguson's e-mail sleight-of-hand had been played out in *RISKS*, AIS still clung gamely to its reputation. It took a serendipitous fax from the House of Representatives' Committee on Space, Technology and Science requesting a copy of the *RISKS* issue in question to panic bureaucrats above Clancy at the Bureau of the Public Debt. Although the requestor was never identified and no follow-up ensued, managers worried that the sky was falling—surely a congressional investigation was imminent.

Calling a meeting to discuss the future of AIS BBS, managers thrust aside arguments from Clancy that removing the hacker files and code from the BBS would only shoot security workers in the foot, depriving the less-experienced among them of a source of information and techniques already widely available throughout the U.S. to any 15-year-old with a modem and a minimal understanding of the word 'BBSing.' Her rationale eerily mirrored the same arguments Hans Braun had made while defending his COMSEC system's distribution of *40 Hex* magazine almost a year earlier.

All the hacker files were subsequently removed from AIS BBS and there were no further developments until the story crashed into the national press on June 19. The *Washington Post* ran a front-page story on AIS's virus code and the Associated Press immediately picked it up as "Dial-A-Virus" and sent the news around the world with a savagely inaccurate lead that proclaimed the bulletin board system had aided computer vandals.

The *Post* story was written by Joel Garreau, an experienced reporter who worked for the paper's Style section and who had two well-received books—*The Nine Nations of North America* and *Edge City*, neither of them about computers— under his belt. The *Post* stumbled in its presentation of the facts, failing to tell readers that Ferguson was the "anonymous" from the original *RISKS* letter. Instead, Garreau portrayed Ferguson as providing independent, unbiased testimony corroborating the *RISKS* view of the situation. Ferguson played this double role on the pages of *The Washington Post* to the max, pontificating on the public shame of virus code and hacker tools on a government BBS where any taxpayer could see and download them. "That's like leaving a loaded gun around and people saying, 'It's not my fault if someone picks it up and shoots himself in the head with it,'" he said.

Even John Buchanan tried to get into the act. He read Garreau's story in *The Washington Post* and called the reporter, inviting Garreau to call the Black Axis virus exchange for an education on the ins and outs of virus bulletin boards. Garreau called, but left apparently unimpressed.

Kim Clancy's reputation, for the moment, was toast, thrown into the barnyard muck and trampled by anti-virus software developer-manipulated rabble from the newsmedia too easily convinced that an out-of-control government agency had been subverted by hackers into working for the forces of darkness. An official reality had been created, one that had Clancy and The Bureau of Public Debt smeared as morally bankrupt, according to one piece by columnist Wayne Rash which appeared in the specialty tabloid, *Communications Week.*[3]

The charges and countercharges flew in the *Computer underground Digest*, where Ferguson became a lightning rod for the ire of Clancy's supporters. From the outside, it must have looked like nothing if not a wilderness of mirrors, completely blinding and stupefying to those who didn't know much about the principals.

The AIS scandal, of course, would not have been complete without a puffed-up Congressman, outraged by *The Washington Post* expose, contributing his two cents. Rep. Edward Markey, Democratic chairman of the House Subcommittee on Telecommunications and Finance, fired off a long, rambling letter of protest to Secretary of the Treasury Lloyd Bentsen.

Markey was, perhaps, the only man for this job since he had established himself as something of a Congressional expert on the information highway by dint of his position astride the House subcommittee most likely to be drafting any and all preliminary legislation concerning it. Markey was also a glutton for media attention. In July 1988, *Washingtonian* magazine published a poll dubbing him the "No. 1 'Camera Hog' in Congress." Writing a stormy letter to the Secretary of the Treasury was, for Markey, who

---

3   Wayne Rash, "Government-sponsored system-cracking lessons are on-line", *Communications Week*, June 28, 1993.

was actually only vaguely familiar with AIS, another natural publicity op. In part, it read:

> "I am writing with regard to recent reports about a computer bulletin board service run under the auspices of the Department's Bureau of Public Debt in Parkersburg, W.V. The Washington Post reported on June 19, 1993, that the now-terminated service made publicly available information about computer viruses and other 'hacker' information that could potentially inflict damage on computer systems and data . . . While it is true that many such virus programs as well as hacker and 'phone phreak' information is available on other bulletin board systems, I am troubled that the Treasury Department would play a role in disseminating such information publicly, especially in light of the fact that viruses and toll fraud together are estimated to inflict $4 to $6 Billion in economic loss annually to U.S. consumers and industry. Such dissemination goes well beyond any precautionary security measure the Department might take in testing the integrity of its computer systems."

This made the AIS situation appear as if Clancy had no colleagues who believed as she did; that she was one loose cannon who had slipped her gun mount and was now careening around threatening to crush the feet of the innocent and unwitting in mainstream computing. This was hardly the case, but the only place Clancy's defenders could get into print to say so was in *Computer underground Digest*, and *CuD*, unfortunately, was not exactly the kind of publication one found on Joe Slob's front porch every morning.

Nevertheless, Jim Thomas, editor of the digest and a professor at Northern Illinois University where it originated, took up the cudgel with others to defend Clancy in issue 5.51

AIS was a reputable and professionally run open-access system, wrote Thomas. It had one of the most comprehensive collections of text and software related to all aspects of security in the country. Thomas recognized that there was the natural inclination of some to object to these materials, but the actions of Ferguson, Solomon and others, in the aggregate, was to present the controversial information "out of context" for the purposes of "piecing together an image of immorality or worse . . ."

"That the accusers [made] their claims while hiding behind the cloak of anonymity strikes me as the type of cowardice associated with witch hunts," wrote Thomas. The opponents of AIS seemed "to be part of a handful of strident pseudo-moral entrepreneurs who feel that only the information they judge as appropriate for public consumption should be made available."

Thomas also tackled Ferguson head on, accusing him of duplicity and maintaining that the "whistleblower" had misrepresented himself as a member of the on-line rights organizations Computer Professionals for Social Responsibility and the Electronic Frontier Foundation.

Frank Tirado, a computer security specialist at the U.S. Department of Agriculture, weighed in on the side of Clancy and AIS. Paul Melka, a corporate computer security expert, pointed out that the information on AIS was of little use to "budding virus writers" because there were already a large number of private systems that were easier for them to access.

AIS, said Melka, provided a "neutral area" where security workers and hackers could meet. In addition, a large number of anti-virus professionals were listed in the system's user registry. "If [AIS] is so tainted, what are all these respected professionals doing on the board?" he mused.

Although little, if any, of this made it into the mainstream media, the pressure was apparently getting to Ferguson. Shortly after being torn apart in the pages of *CuD* and *The Crypt Newsletter*, he sent me vaguely menacing electronic mail:

```
Your literary skills leave much to be desired,
but nontheless [sic], are still rather amusing.
I hope you don't expect many folks to take your
CRYPT editorials too seriously, but you do have
a right to express your opinion in any fashion
you choose.

This is protected under the 1st Amendment, no
matter how much you or I may dislike it. Put
that in your pipe and smoke on it for while
[sic], or at least until the other shoe drops.

Cheerio.
Paul Ferguson
```

Ferguson also replied to his attackers in *CuD* 5.52. He insisted he believed in freedom of information but that he was partial to this interpretation of the concept: "The freedom to swing your fist ends where it meets my face."

And, Ferguson bullishly claimed, he would defend to the death the rights of those who wished to disagree with him. However, supporters of systems like AIS were to be dismissed. They were either ignorant of the real facts about viruses, radicals or loud-mouths.

As for AIS, "Now that I think about about it again, I'm really not sorry," he wrote.

Eventually, the scandal died although from time to time a sanctimonious member of CARO would blindside Clancy in the comp.virus echo on the Internet. Fridrik Skulason insinuated months later that Clancy's system had been responsible for the Secret Service's network being knocked off-line by Satan Bug because Little Loc had contributed his virus's source code to the original AIS database.

Whenever the names Ferguson, Skulason or Solomon came up in polite conversation with Clancy, she would sneer and bark, "Anti-virus experts, I hate 'em."

In the long run, the affair made Clancy a kind of Joan of Arc figure in the computer underground. She continued to lecture around the country on network security and began teaching a class on computer viruses at a regional college. Some of the computer underground material she had collected on AIS was turned into a chapter in a book on network computer security written by anti-virus researcher David Stang. The book, *Network Security Secrets*[4] won a minor award for its publisher, International Data Group, in San Mateo, California.

As for Paul Ferguson, he withdrew as moderator of his virus information echo on the FIDO-net, handing it over to the American representative of yet another European anti-virus software firm. In May 1994 Ferguson popped up again, this time as a guest editorial writer for the virus-writing magazine *40 Hex*[5], the same *40 Hex* which had been part of the material he objected to on AIS.

---

4 David Stang & Sylvia Moon, *Network Security Secrets*, IDG Books, 1993.

"The intents and conceptions of the AIS may have been noble and genuine; I believe this to be the case," Ferguson wrote. "In fact, I commend Kim Clancy . . . on her efforts in the computer and telecommunications security arena."

When Clancy saw it, she laughed. "Can you believe him?" she roared. Paul Ferguson was one very strange bird.

---

5   Paul Ferguson, "Guest editorial", *40 Hex* (Hardcopy), May, 1994.

The Toymaker and the Toad

About the same time Kim Clancy was having so much fun with the members of CARO, another American named Doren Rosenthal was about to tangle with the same nest of vipers for daring to enter the anti-virus business.

Doren Rosenthal was a toymaker living in San Luis Obispo, California. With degrees in electronics and computer science from California Polytechnic and California State at Northridge, the bearish Rosenthal had been working as an inventor for twenty years, first in Southern California's San Fernando Valley and later along its scenic central coast.

His most famous invention was the P. J. Sparkles doll, a Mattel toy which bewitched little girls across the nation when it was marketed just before the 1989 Christmas season. Rosenthal had designed the electronics that controlled the array of sparkling lights embedded in the doll's earrings, bracelet, hair bow and heart. He had even programed the software simulation of P. J. Sparkles which was used to sell Mattel executives on the idea. Rosenthal liked nothing better than to invent toys for small children. His eyes lit up when showing off P. J. Sparkles and other toys which he collected as a sideline.

Doren Rosenthal had heard that I was interested in viruses and invited me to stop by his home while en route from Pasadena to a conference in San Francisco during the summer of 1993. He said he was always looking for new projects and had developed some products which he thought might fit into the anti-virus industry.

When I arrived in San Luis Obispo, Rosenthal first insisted on showing me the town and some of its more peculiar attractions. One of these was The Chewing Gum Wall, a narrow downtown alley encrusted from street level to rooftop with already-been-chewed chewing gum. Quite frankly, The Chewing Gum Wall was way beyond disgusting, but the locals had inventively tried to turn it into a kind of cultural monument.

Another of San Luis Obispo's bizarre tourist attractions was located in the basement of The Madonna Motel and Restaurant. Rosenthal rushed me into The Madonna's men's room, which turned out to be equipped with a sculpted clamshell group urinal armed with an infrared sensor. When you whipped it out, a waterfall cascaded down the back of the clamshell. It was, uh, truly high-tech and as Rosenthal laughed and showed it to me I was seized with the sneaking suspicion that he had designed the electronics for it.

Four years earlier, Rosenthal said, he'd started fooling around with the development of software useful for system monitoring. Out of this, he identified a need for the testing of anti-virus scanners without the use of thousands of live viruses. As one answer, he produced a program he called the Virus Simulator, a small piece of software which merely spat out dummy do-nothing programs embedded with markers Rosenthal extracted from viruses. Ideally, it was these same virus markers, or strings of instructions, that the best anti-virus scanners would look for.

At first, Rosenthal said, developers like McAfee were interested. They saw it as an easy way for prospective buyers to test-drive their software. However, the initial attitude quickly soured. By the fall of 1991, few developers would cooperate with Rosenthal. He saw this as a fear on the part of anti-virus sellers who didn't actually want anyone to test their software independently, with dummy files or live viruses, period. The reliability of virus detectors was a matter of image rather than fact, Rosenthal thought. Scanners were rarely genuinely tested by independents. The consumer was relied upon to make a big leap of faith as to their accuracy.

Rosenthal steamed ahead. With the first edition of the Virus Simulator in the market, vendors who had shunned him initially now called to hector him about why he hadn't included their virus scan strings in the simulator. CARO member Fridrik Skulason was one of these types. He had contacted Rosenthal, the inventor said, to chastise him for not including signatures specific to Skulason's anti-virus software in the simulator. Underlying the perturbation in the anti-virus industry was the fear that not only might Rosenthal's simple program shake consumer confidence, but worse, if successful, it could force developers to include the Virus Simulator's scan strings in their programs, too, lest they appear ineffective when tested against it.

But Rosenthal had bigger ideas. He wanted to develop the Virus Simulator even further and interest someone in buying his ideas and software for a protection scheme he called Virus Armor. Rosenthal wanted in to CARO, too.

CARO's Alan Solomon seemed receptive to the idea, said Rosenthal, but he thought that tricky Fridrik Skulason was blackballing him.

"I like the idea of anti-virus software," said Rosenthal. "You can sell a subscription to it. That's appealing."

During the winter of 1992, Rosenthal updated his Virus Simulator with something called the MtE Supplement. The MtE Supplement produced controlled viruses which fielded the Mutation Engine. They would only infect dummy files produced by the Virus Simulator, and so Rosenthal reasoned, were quite safe to use when testing anti-virus scanners for effectiveness against Mutation Engine polymorphism.

But, as might be expected, Rosenthal was immediately declared a menace by CARO member Vesselin Vladimirov Bontchev. Posting publicly in the Usenet's comp.virus newsgroup, Bontchev declared:

```
Either the simulator is useless, or you are dis-
tributing malicious software . . . Hmmm, I was
able to draw this conclusion even without hav-
ing to look at the simulator . . . pretty good,
isn't it?
```

Bontchev, like many other people involved in the world of computer viruses, had a curious history. In the late Eighties, the Bulgarian had been toiling as a writer for a computer magazine in Sofia, Bulgaria. According to the book *Approaching Zero* by Paul Mungo and Bryan Clough, he and a friend by the name of Teodor Prevalsky became interested in computer viruses.

Their setup worked something like this: Prevalsky would program a virus and hand it over to Bontchev, who would write about it. Acting as a *de facto* mouthpiece for the work of Prevalsky, Bontchev would publicize the virus to the world while establishing his cards as an expert on the programs. One of the first viruses to appear out of this convention was a program-infecting virus which played the tune "Yankee Doodle." It was a very simple .EXE-program-infecting virus whose source code was emblazoned with the name "Vladimir Botchev." Bontchev, who wrote about the virus programed by someone with a name so strangely like his own insisted it was not his doing. According to Mungo and Clough, the Bulgarian turned the virus—eventually named "Old Yankee"—right over to his friend Prevalsky, who began cranking out variants of it which subsequently became known as the TP or Yankee Doodle series of viruses. Eventually, these viruses found their way into a collection known as "the Bulgarian 50," which was released to the West around 1990. Prevalsky, wrote Bontchev in a widely distributed samizdat monograph entitled "The Bulgarian and Soviet Virus Factories," just accidentally, heh-heh, infected other people's computer disks where he worked with the TP viruses. These viruses, along with others and their source codes, some of the analyses with Bontchev's name on them, would also just accidentally, heh-heh, wind up on virus exchange bulletin board systems run by teenagers in the United States.

Although Prevalsky apparently stopped writing the majority of Bulgarian viruses, Vesselin Bontchev quickly discovered another countryman to take the place of his colleague. This time Bontchev took up flacking for the Dark Avenger, who with a push from Vesselin, eventually went on to gain the weird reputation as the world's greatest virus writer. Although the Dark Avenger never publicly stepped forward, Bontchev wrote and talked about the Avenger's viruses, ones with names like Number of the Beast and, typically, Dark Avenger.

Bontchev was also occasionally dogged by accusations that he was the Dark Avenger. He wasn't, he insisted. In 1993 in an interview conducted by electronic mail and published in the March issue of S&S International's *Virus News International*, the Dark Avenger called Bontchev a "weasel."[1] The Dark Avenger strongly resented Bontchev's coat-tailing, claiming the Bulgarian had exacerbated the virus problems he was chronicling by goading others into writing them as technical challenges. Surprisingly, the Dark Avenger also named Bontchev as a virus writer, maintaining, "... his viruses were pretty worthless. He is not a good programmer." Weirdly, the Dark Avenger contradicted himself in the same interview by insisted that Bontchev's articles were great guides to virus writing but, "I'm not saying that he wrote them himself, though." Yep, this was the same Bontchev who called Doren Rosenthal a programmer of malicious code before even inspecting the toymaker's software.

Rosenthal was very irritated. He stormed back at the Bulgarian:

```
I'm disappointed that you would pass yourself
off as a fair and open scientist and researcher
open to new ideas. Then . . . without even exam-
ining the Virus Simulator MtE Supplement your-
self, draw a conclusion and announce your
findings in a public forum.
```

However, Rosenthal was still determined to join CARO. He became convinced Alan Solomon held the key because the Englishman had been friendly to him. Rosenthal asked what I thought of the situation.

I told him I had just finished doing a product review of Alan Solomon's Antivirus Toolkit and that it had detected Rosenthal's MtE Simulator programs as "Doren Rosenthal" viruses. When you looked up the "Doren Rosenthal" virus in the Toolkit's on-line virus encyclopedia, you were told these viruses weren't in the wild but "they could be." I said it didn't look like Alan Solomon was programming his software to cooperate with Rosenthal's MtE Supplement and that, in any case, the virus encyclopedia had named Rosenthal a virus writer by default. On the face of it, it sure didn't look like Rosenthal would be joining CARO anytime soon. The inventor remained nonplussed.

Besides the Virus Simulator and its add-ons, Rosenthal was also trying to sell his ideas for an anti-virus software suite called Virus Armor. He had hired an intern from California Polytechnic

---

1   Sara Gordon, "Dedicated", *Virus News International*, February, 1993.

and together they had gotten down to the work of programming anti-virus software which could be incorporated with Microsoft Windows executables. The Virus Armor software would, ideally, be applied to Windows applications and programs by software engineers who had licensed it for use. Then the "immunized" software would be shipped. The consumer would purchase the Virus Armor-treated programs, install them on his machine and whenever the new program was executed, Virus Armor would fire up, check its host program for changes and call a scanner from within the library of Windows resources which would quickly search the system for known viruses. If a virus was found, or changes made by an unknown virus detected, Virus Armor would halt and sound the alarm, making it impossible for viruses to flourish on a protected system. The tricky part, said the inventor, was writing all the Virus Armor software in assembly language segments and then getting it into Windows programs without disrupting anything. Virus Armor had to be fast and not add anything very noticeable to the already flabby Windows software. In fact, the Virus Armor treatment also compressed Windows applications, making them take up less space on a computer's hard disk. Programming it had almost given the intern a nervous break-down, laughed Rosenthal.

Symantec, thought Rosenthal, might be interested in Virus Armor. So he called his brother, who was a hot-shot lawyer in Beverly Hills, to arrange a meeting and demonstration with Symantec representatives who had the power to "put some money on the table."

According to Rosenthal, the Symantec reps were impressed but noncommittal. Virus Armor rendered the current edition of Symantec's anti-virus software, the Norton Antivirus, obsolete and that wasn't exactly what the company had in mind, said Rosenthal. Symantec wasn't ready to junk the Norton Antivirus.

While this may have been true, there were other reasons why Virus Armor never really flew, despite the fact it was flashy and appeared to work as advertised. Primary among these was that the licensing of Virus Armor, quite simply, would have been akin to selling ice to Eskimos. At the time Rosenthal developed Virus Armor there simply were no viruses that effectively infected Windows. Masud Khafir of the Dutch virus-writing group Trident had tried his hand at one, but it didn't really work. Viruses that operated on a machine with Windows installed either stayed away from the software, or were boot sector infectors which operated underneath the Windows shell, independent of that overlaid operating system. In any case, they were the same old PC-compatible system viruses as usual and DOS antivirus software was sufficient to control them. Unruly DOS viruses that got into Windows programs either immediately crashed the system, prevented Windows applications from working or didn't replicate. Ironically, this made Windows itself a very sensitive screen for virus presence, no add-ons necessary.

Rosenthal appeared to grasp this in a vague manner. Programming Virus Armor had made him intimately familiar with how a virus might be written to effectively attack Windows. However, in his estimation, American virus writers were either too stupid or lacked the patience to program them. The only computer programmers with the skill were in Europe, said Rosenthal. But the Europeans didn't really like Windows, so it was unlikely, he thought, that they would ever get down to the task of writing viruses targeting it.

Although Rosenthal patented Virus Armor,[2] it foundered.

This left Rosenthal with the Virus Simulator and a handful of related programs which could be marketed as shareware. Shareware authorship also appealed to the inventor. You could cast your programs upon the ocean of the Internet and with a little good publicity, the cash would begin rolling right back to you as users began to send in registration fees. No middleman or formal advertising necessary!

The only problem with this plan was that the rascal Vesselin Bontchev had so tarred Rosenthal's reputation with his Internet flame that the administrators of the Internet shareware sites where Rosenthal wanted to distribute his programs were skittish. They didn't want to be blamed for spreading Rosenthal's "malicious software," even though it was perfectly harmless. CARO membership might help in overturning this obstacle. Rosenthal was still stubbornly determined to gain entrance into the elite club.

It never happened. However, months later the inventor was finally able to distribute his Simulator through the Internet. But

---

2 U.S. Patent no. 5,359,659, issued October, 1994.

Rosenthal had changed his mind about CARO and Alan Solomon. He wasn't interested in group membership anymore and as for Solomon, Rosenthal said the English antivirus expert had just stabbed him in the back. Rosenthal had been using a European academic from Bratislava, Peter Hubinsky, to collect viruses and sort a collection the toymaker had been maintaining. Solomon had gotten wind of this and persuaded Hubinsky to screw Rosenthal, cutting off the American in return for promises of access to Solomon's virus samples and blandishments about possible CARO membership.

Paradoxically, two years later, virus writers—- who, according to Bontchev, would have been interested in perverting Rosenthal's "malicious software" for their own uses—- still showed not the slightest interest in the MtE simulation viruses. Not only didn't they need Rosenthal's simulation as a source for the Mutation Engine, but most who were moved to write polymorphic viruses were using their own engines, not a buggy one which had been so well publicized that even the poorest anti-virus software at least pretended to detect it.

As for Vesselin Bontchev, his vainglory as some kind of Internet-inhabiting virus guru had inflated to the point where his cyber-persona on comp.virus resembled that of an odious and puffed-up toad. Ensconced at the University of Hamburg in Germany where he analyzed computer virus after computer virus and evaluated and re-evaluated the same six or seven anti-virus programs over and over, Bontchev witlessly argued with everyone who didn't agree with him on comp.virus until the Usenet conference on the Internet became ossified and claustrophobic. According to Rosenthal, the moderator of the newsgroup, Ken van Wyk, was essentially a cyberflunky of the Bulgarian.

In public electronic mail, Bontchev would self-pityingly complain about how fighting the scourge of the wicked computer viruses was making him ill:

```
So, what is exactly my interest in this? Per-
haps you think that I am a masochist (sp?), en-
joying working 14 hours per day on a half-time
job, ruining my health, and replying to stupid
questions?
```

And, despite the passage of time, in mid-1994 the "boorish" Bulgarian, as Paskell Paris dubbed him, was still madly barking at Doren Rosenthal, like a neurotic dog left too long in an empty house. However, this time it wasn't only Rosenthal's simulated Mutation Engine viruses that were malicious, it was the toymaker's harmless virus dummies, too. Why, it was everything about Rosenthal the Bulgarian disliked: his software, his ideas, his intelligence, perhaps even the color of his shirt!

"[Doren Rosenthal's] so-called 'virus simulator' is *completely* useless for testing anti-virus software," wrote Bontchev in July 1994 on comp.virus. "The 'simulated viruses' generated by it are not viruses at all—just collections of scan strings stollen [sic] from different scanners . . . In short—completely useless product, and a harmful one too, because it misleads the people."

Bontchev continued his psychotic typewritten attack throughout the late summer of 1994. Rosenthal, claimed Bontchev, was originally making the Mutation Engine simulator available due to "simple incompetence." But now, Bontchev was certain the inventor was marketing evil code "intentionally and with malicious intent in mind . . ."

". . . you, [Rosenthal], are a virus writer and distributor," gibbered the Bulgarian.

These repetitive screeds created the substantial impression that Ken van Wyk allowed the comp.virus newsgroup to be an arena where his colleagues could libel anyone they didn't care for without fear of reprisal. Simply, there was not a shred of evidence to support the claim that Doren Rosenthal had ever created anything for malicious use in his career as an inventor and programmer of software.

To his credit, Doren Rosenthal no longer let the crazed outbursts of Vesselin Bontchev bug him. "It's just not worth it," he laughed. "Besides, the Virus Simulator is more popular now than it was four years ago."

However, in the screwed-up world of Vesselin Bontchev and the Usenet's comp.virus newsgroup, Doren Rosenthal had found you couldn't win for losing.

A Priest Deploys his Satanic Minions

Everyone knows the best virus writers hang out on secret bulletin board systems, the bedroom bohemias of the computer underground, right? Wrong. In mid-1992, a 16-year-old hacker from San Diego who called himself Little Loc signed on to the Prodigy on-line service for his virus information needs. The experience was not quite what he expected.

Prodigy had a reputation in 1992 as the on-line service for middle-class Americans who could stand mind-roasting amounts of retail advertising on their computer screens as long as they had relatively free access to an almost infinite number of public electronic mail forums devoted to callers' hobbies. Since Prodigy's pricing scheme was ridiculously cheap per hour, it was quite seductive for callers to spend an hour or two a night sifting through endless strings of messages just to engage in a little cyberspace chit-chat.

Into this living-room atmosphere stepped Little Loc, logged on as James Gentile, looking for anyone to talk with about computer viruses, particularly his idea of properly written computer viruses. Little Loc, you see, had written a polymorphic virus which infected most of the programs on a system dangerously quickly. If you were using anti-virus software that didn't properly recognize the virus—and at the time it was written none did—the very process of looking for it on a machine would spread it to every possible program on a computer's hard disk. While many viruses were trivial toys, Satan

Bug, which is what Little Loc called his program, was sophisticated enough to pose a real hazard. The trouble was, Little Loc was dying to tell people about Satan Bug. But he had no one to talk to who would understand. That's where Prodigy came in. Prodigy, thought Little Loc, must have some hacker discussions, even if they were feeble, centered on viruses. It was a quaintly naïve assumption.

The Satan Bug was named after a seventies telemovie starring George Maharis, Anne Francis and a sinister Richard Basehart in a race to find a planet-sterilizing super-virus stolen from a U.S. bio-warfare lab. Little Loc had never actually seen the movie, but he'd run across the name in a copy of *TV Guide* and it sounded cool, so he used it for his digital creation. Satan Bug was the second virus he had electronically published. The first was named Fruitfly, and it, too, was polymorphic like Satan Bug, but it was a slow, tame infector so the hacker didn't push it.

A bigger inspiration for Satan Bug was the work of the Dark Avenger, the shadowy Bulgarian virus programmer whom Vesselin Bontchev and others had elevated to the stature of world's greatest virus writer. Little Loc was fascinated by the viruses attributed to Dark Avenger. The Dark Avenger obviously knew how real computer viruses should be written, thought Little Loc. None of his programs were like the silly crap that composed most of the files stocked by the computer underground. For example, the Crazy Eddie virus—also known as Dark Avenger—had gained a reputation as a program to be reckoned with. It pushed fast infection to a fine art, using the very process anti-virus programs used to examine files as an opportunity to corrupt them with its presence. If someone suspected they had a virus, scanned for it and Crazy Eddie was in memory but not detected, the anti-virus software would be subverted, spreading Crazy Eddie to every program on the disk in one sweep. Crazy Eddie would also mangle a part of the machine's command shell when it jumped into memory from an infected program. When this happened, the command processor would reload itself from the hard disk and promptly be infected, too. This put the Eddie virus in total charge of the machine. From that point on, every sixteen infections, the virus would take a pot shot at a sector of the hard disk, obliterating a small piece of data. If the data were part of a never-used program, it could go unnoticed. So as long as the Eddie virus was in command, the user stood a good chance of having to deal with a slow, creeping corruption of his programs and data.

Little Loc was a good student of the Dark Avenger's programming and although he was completely self-taught, he had more native ability than all of the virus programmers in phalcon/SKISM and NuKE. "[Virus writing] was something to do besides blasting furballs in Wing Commander," he said blithely when asked about the origins of his career as a virtuoso virus writer.

Accordingly, the Satan Bug was just as fast an infector as Crazy Eddie and it, too, would immediately go after the command shell when launched into memory from an infected program. But Satan Bug was polymorphic, too, and it extended its encryption tricks so that it was cloaked in computer memory, a feature somewhat unusual in computer viruses but popularized by another virus called The Whale which intrigued Little Loc.

The Whale was a German virus which was the most complex of all computer viruses written to date. It was packed with code which was supposed to make it stealthy—invisible to certain anti-virus software techniques. It was polymorphic and was armed with anti-debugging code designed purely to flummox anti-virus software developers trying to examine it. They would often mention it as an example of a super stealth virus to mystified science and technology writers looking for good copy. In practice, The Whale was what one might call anti-stealth. Although it was all the things mentioned and more, when run on any machine, The Whale's processes were so cumbersome the computer would be forced to slow to a crawl.

The Whale appeared to be purely an intellectual challenge for programmers. It was intended to mesmerize anti-virus software developers and suck them into spending hours analyzing it. Little Loc, too, was drawn to it. He pored over the German language disassembly of The Whale's source code. The hacker even made a version that wasn't encrypted, pulling out the code which The Whale used to generate its score of mutant polymorphic variations. It didn't help. The Whale, even when disassembled, was loathe to let go of its secrets and remained a slow, obstinately uninfective puzzle.

Have you gotten the idea that Prodigy callers might not be the perfect choice as an audience to appreciate Little Loc's Satan Bug?

Nevertheless, Little Loc landed on Prodigy with a thud. He described the Satan Bug and invited anyone who was interested to pick up a copy of its source code at a bulletin board system where he'd stashed it. Immediately, the hacker got into a rhubarb with a Prodigy member named Henri Delger. Delger was, for want of a better description, the Prodigy network's unpaid computer virus help desk manager. Every night, Delger would log on and look for the messages of users who had questions about computer viruses. If they just wanted general information, Delger would supply it. If they had some kind of computer glitch which they thought might be a virus, Delger would hold their hand until they calmed down, and then tell them what to do. And, for the few who had computer virus infections, Delger would try to identify the virus and recommend software, usually McAfee Associates' SCAN, which would remedy the problem.

Little Loc was annoyed by Delger, whom he thought was merely a shill for McAfee Associates. Since Delger answered so many questions on Prodigy, he had a set of canned answers which he would employ to make the workload lighter. The canned answers tended to antagonize Little Loc and other younger callers who fancied themselves hackers, too. Prodigy's liberal demo account policy allowed some of these young callers to get access to the network under assumed names like "Orion Rogue." This allowed them to be rude and truculent, at least for a few days, to paying Prodigy customers. These techno-popinjays, of course, immediately sided with Little Loc, which didn't do much for the virus programmer's credibility.

There was often quite a bit of talk about viruses and Delger would supply much of the information, typing up brief summaries of virus effects embroidered with his own experiences analyzing viruses. "You're not a programmer!" Little Loc would storm at Delger. "If you aren't a programmer, you can't understand viruses," insisted the author of Satan Bug. Little Loc would correct minor technical errors Delger made when describing the programs. In retaliation, Delger would calmly point out the spelling mistakes made by Little Loc and his colleagues. It was quite a flame war. On one side was Little Loc, who gamely tried to get callers to appreciate the technical qualities of some viruses. On the other side was a bunch of middle-aged computer hobbyists who were convinced all virus writers were illiterate teenage nincompoops in need of serious jail time, or perhaps a sound beating.

The debates drew a big audience, including another hacker named Brian Oblivion, whose Waco, Texas, bulletin board, Caustic Contagion, would provide a brief haven for Satan Bug's author. Little Loc, however, soon found other places that would accept his virus source code. Kim Clancy's Department of the Treasury Security Branch system was among them. Little Loc logged on and contributed Satan Bug. Hell Pit's phone number was posted on Prodigy, as was that of Tim Caton's Dark Coffin. Dutifully, Little Loc couriered his virus to these systems, too.

I also received a copy of the virus from the hacker. It came with source code, an instruction file and a pre-assembled copy of the virus. In part, it looked much like this:

```
Little Loc—0293

Hacker4Life!

Please upload this to as many BBS's as possible!
Although I created this virus, I will hold no
copyright on it—feel free to modify and improve
it.

Files included:
SAT-BUG.ASM (Assembly source code)
SAT-BUG.COM (Assembled virus)
TEST1.COM (Program infected with virus)

To get the infection going follow these
instructions: (If you're rather computer dumb
just follow the commands after the dashes)

1. Make backup of COMMAND.COM
—COPY C:\COMMAND.COM C:\COMMAND.BAK

2. Execute included file TEST1.COM (It is
already infected)
—test1.COM
```

3. Execute program to be infected
—C:\INFECTED.COM
(Do not use C:\INFECTED.COM. Instead replace
that parameter with that of a program you have
on your computer and the path it is in), i.e.
C:\DOS\DISKCOPY

4. Disinfect COMMAND.COM
—COPY C:\COMMAND.BAK COMMAND.COM

5. Clear virus from memory—Hit red switch on
back of computer

BE CAREFUL—VIRUS SPREADS RAPIDLY AND MOSTLY
UNNOTICED!

If it spreads on your computer, your up
a certain creek without a padle, although
the virus will not do any damage, no
scanning program will find this virus
and thus EVERY FILE ON YOUR COMPUTER COULD
EVENTUALLY BECOME INFECTED!

And no, you can not put a string into a file
and use Scan with the /EXT switch, since there
are no constant strings in a polymorphic virus
of such.

From: USA!

I'M GONNA STRIKE AGAIN!

Satan Bug was a difficult virus to scan. Although in a pinch you
could find Satan Bug because of a trick change it made to an
infected program's date/time stamp, for all intents and purposes
Satan Bug was transparent to anti-virus scanners. And this window
of opportunity stayed open for a surprising amount of time despite
the fact that Little Loc had supplied the Satan Bug to all the public
virus exchanges patrolled by anti-virus moles.

Little Loc stood apart from other virus programmers who
seemed to have little interest in whether their creations made it into
the public's computers. The real travel of his virus around the world

would grant him recognition like that of the Dark Avenger, he thought. So, he wanted people to take Satan Bug and infect the software of others, period. Months later, after the virus had struck down the Secret Service network clear across the continent, I asked Little Loc how it might have gotten into the wild in large enough numbers so that it eventually found its way into such a supposedly secure system.

"I'll tell you this once and only once: Satan Bug had help!" he said, simply.

After his Prodigy debut and before Satan Bug hit the Secret Service, Little Loc was recruited by phalcon/SKISM, changing his handle in the process to Priest. Joining phalcon/SKISM didn't necessarily mean you were going to virus writing conventions in cyberspace with other members of the group, but it was a badge of status signifying to others in the computer underground who required such things that you had arrived, as a virus writer anyway.

Since Priest lived on the West Coast, however, and the brain trust of phalcon/SKISM was located in the metro-NYC area, there was little concrete collaboration between the two, especially after Priest racked up a $600 telephone bill calling bulletin boards. Since Priest didn't hack free phone service, his family had to pay the bill, which effectively cut down on much of his telephone contact with places like Black Axis and Caustic Contagion in Waco, Texas.

Caustic Contagion, for a short period of time, was one of the better known virus exchange bulletin board systems. Its sysop, Brian Oblivion, had an extremely liberal policy with regards to virus access and carried a large number of Internet/Usenet newsgroups which gave callers a semblance of access to the Internet. Caustic Contagion's other specialty, besides viruses, was Star Trek newsgroups and for some reason which completely eludes me, the BBS's callers found the convergence of computer viruses and Star Trek debate extremely congenial.

Priest and another phalcon/SKISM virus writer named Memory Lapse would hang out on Caustic Contagion. Quite naturally, Oblivion's bulletin board was one of the first places to receive the programmers' newest creations, often before they were published in *40 Hex* magazine.

Priest's next virus was Payback and it was written to punish the mainstream computing community for the arrest of Apache Warrior, the "president" of ARCV, the English virus-writing group. The virus would format the hard disk in memory of this event. Payback gathered little attention in the underground, mostly because few people knew much about ARCV and Apache Warrior in the first place.

Another of Priest's interests was the set of anti-virus programs issued by the Dutch company, Thunderbyte. The product of a virus researcher named Frans Veldman, the Thunderbyte programs were regarded by most virus writers as the anti-virus programs of choice. They were sophisticated, technically sweet and put to shame similar software marketed by McAfee Associates, Central Point Software, and Symantec, which manufactured the Norton Anti-virus.

One of Frans Veldman's programs, called TBClean, was of particular interest to Priest and others because it claimed to be able to remove completely unknown viruses from infected files. How it did this was a neat trick. Essentially, TBClean would execute the virus-infected file in a controlled environment and try to take advantage of the fact that the virus always had to reassemble in memory an uncontaminated copy of the infected program to make it work properly. TBClean would intercept this action and write the program back to the hard disk sans virus. Priest and virus writer Rock Steady, who had also noticed the phenomenon, tried writing viruses that would subvert the process and turn TBClean upon itself.

Priest wrote Jackal, a virus which—under the proper conditions—would sense TBClean trying to execute it, step outside the Thunderbyte software's controls and format the hard disk. In theory, this made Priest's virus the worst kind of retaliating program, with the potential to destructively strip unsuspecting users' hard disks of their data when they tried to disinfect their machines. (It couldn't happen if you just manually erased the Jackal-virus-infected program, but many people who use computers as part of everyday work simply want the option of having the software remove viruses. They don't want to have to worry about the technicalities of retaliating viruses designed to smash their data if they have the temerity to use anti-virus software.)

Of course, Jackal's development was deemed a great propaganda victory by the North American virus underground. Rock Steady nonsensically insisted Frans Veldman's programs were dangerous software because TBClean could be made to augment a virus infection instead of remove it.

Brian Oblivion immediately tried Jackal out. It didn't work, he said, but only caused TBClean to hang up his machine. This was because Jackal was version specific, explained Priest. It would only work on certain editions of the program. In reality, this meant that Jackal's retaliating capability posed little threat to typical computer users, who had never heard of the virus-programmer's favorite software, Thunderbyte, much less TBClean. Nevertheless, Priest continued to write the TBClean subverting trick into his viruses, including it in Natas (that's Satan spelled backwards), which eventually got loose in Mexico City in the spring of 1994.

All the routines to format a computer's hard disk and to slowly corrupt data *a là* Crazy Eddie, which Priest had designed the Predator virus to do, made it clear the hacker cared little for any of the finer arguments over the value of computer viruses which were entertained from time to time by denizens of the underground as well as academics. Viruses were for getting your name around, infecting files and destroying data, according to Priest. He just laughed when the topic of ethical or productive uses of computer viruses—such as the study of artificial life—came up.

This was a matter of some annoyance to Dave Goldsmith, the editor of phalcon/SKISM's *40 Hex*. Ever since late 1992, the virus writing group had been trying to cultivate an air of respectability by keeping purely destructive viruses out of the electronic magazine. When interviewed, Goldsmith, also known as Geoff Heap, maintained that phalcon/SKISM was about providing information on computer viruses. To strengthen the claim, Goldsmith began publishing a paper copy of *40 Hex* in late 1993. The paper copy contained interviews, editorials and some anti-virus product reviews not always republished in the electronic edition of the magazine.

Priest was blowing this plan up, thought Goldsmith, with viruses like Jackal, Predator and Natas, which was published in *40 Hex* #12.[1] All of the programs destroyed data in a purposeful manner, which was not what phalcon/SKISM wanted to be about. No doubt about it, Priest was a genius, said Goldsmith, but someone had to talk to him about his destructive viruses.

---

1 Hmm . . . not blowing it up too much.

By mid-1994, Goldsmith wanted *40 Hex* to take on a new project, which he envisioned as a small-scale version of the cyberspace rights organization, the Electronic Frontier Foundation, known as EFF. The *40 Hex* group, tentatively named VEFF for Virus Electronic Frontier Foundation, would exist, mused Goldsmith, to provide timely information on the real nature of computer viruses whenever it looked like some media-fueled panic on the subject was picking up steam. But Priest's data destroyers made this community service-based initiative on the part of phalcon/SKISM an awkward proposition.

In any case, by the fall of 1993, after Priest had retired from the Prodigy scene, Satan Bug was generating its own kind of media-fueled panic.

On the Compuserve network, hysterical government employees were posting nonsensical alarums about the virus in the McAfee Associates virus information special interest group.

Here's an example from September:

This just came to me via our WAN e-mail:

The State Department has announced that a new
computer virus has been identified. It has been
named "Satan's Bug" and is targeted at
Government Computer systems. The State Dept.
rep said that the National Security Agency
plans to issue a security alert on this soon.
They are concerned over this virus for the following reasons:

* It is not detectable by most systems
* at best, there is only one system that can detect it but only 75% of the time
* it attacks the command files and locks up
the computer and takes down an entire LAN with
it
* it can travel by LAN, disk, or in a new computer
* they know how it entered the country and
which country started it
* it is extremely complicated—9 levels of encryption

```
*  it is spreading fast

The only good news is . . . it does not destroy
your files, you just cannot access them.

The only clue that it is "eating" your system
is SOMETIMES the automatic dates change to 100
years in the future.

If any more information is confirmed it will be
distributed.
```

Wherever the "confirmed" information about "Satan's Bug" was coming from, it was 100 percent phlogiston. Satan Bug was hardly aimed at government computer systems, it did not "eat" anything and although difficult for many anti-virus programs to scan, the virus could be found on infected systems by making good use of software designed to take a snapshot of the vital statistics of computer files and sound an alarm when these changed, which always happened when Satan Bug added itself to programs. In an emergency, it could be located by looking for the odd change to an infected program's time/date stamp the virus made as a cue in determining which files it had already infected. On a heavily infected corporate network, this may have seemed unappealing, but many consider searching for viruses, even with properly optimized software, an unpleasant job. The time/date stamp clue is apparently where the "100 years in the future" idea came from. Even more amusing was the suspicion that Satan Bug had been inserted on government computers by some undisclosed foreign country, from whence it originated. I suppose, however, some people might consider Southern California a foreign country.

Priest enjoyed reading these kinds of things. His virus was famous, an obvious source of confusion and hysteria.

About the same time, the Secret Service's computer network in Washington, D.C., was infected by the virus, which knocked the infected machines off-line for approximately three days. News about the event was tough to keep secret among government employees and it leaked. *The Crypt Newsletter* published a short news piece in its September 1993 issue on the event and reported that the infection had been cleaned up by David Stang, formerly of the National Computer Security Association, but now providing anti-virus and security guidance for Norman Data Defense Systems in Fairfax, northern Virginia.

Jack Lewis, head of the Secret Service's computer crime unit, and two other agents flew out to interrogate Priest in his San Diego home in October of 1993.

Lewis and the other agents gave Priest the third degree. They shook a printed-out copy of *The Crypt Newsletter* containing the Satan Bug story in his face and did everything in their power to make Priest think he ought to cease and desist writing computer viruses forthwith.

"About the Secret Service, they weren't too happy about [Satan Bug], and saw fit to pay me a little visit," recalled Priest ruefully.

The agents wanted to know everything about Priest—his Social Security number, where he'd travelled, even who the 16-year-old worked for. But Priest didn't work for anyone.

"I'm not quite sure they believed me," he said. "Apparently, they thought I worked for some anti-virus company or something to write viruses. Plus, they wanted the sources for them."

The Secret Service men wanted to know, straight from the horse's mouth, what Satan Bug did. "They said some victims were worried their systems weren't completely clean because they thought it might infect data files," Priest continued. "I told them it wouldn't. They also wanted my opinion on things which surprised me, like different anti-virus programs and encryption algorithms, including Clipper. I didn't ask why.

"Jack Lewis also said someone claimed I said 'All government computers will be infected by December' or some such rubbish. Apparently, they thought I wrote Satan Bug as a weapon against the government or whatever, I can't be too sure . . ."

Priest told them no, Satan Bug wasn't specifically aimed at government computers, but it was hard to tell if the agents believed him. They were trained to reveal little, and to be unnerving to those interviewed.

"They just stared," Priest said, "as they did in response to every question I asked, including 'what's your name?' I tried—really tried—to act cool, but my heart was pounding like a humming-bird's."

The agents were keenly interested in Priest's other handles, all the viruses he had written, which, if any, computer systems he might have spread them on, the names of some phalcon/SKISM members and the structure of the virus-writing group and details of their hacking exploits.

Priest declined to say anything about the identities of members of phalcon/SKISM. "I told them I knew nothing of the hackers and phreakers, and little more than you could pick up from reading an issue of *40 Hex*."

Priest was more interested in other secretive agencies within the government. He cultivated an interest in stories about deep black intelligence agencies. Perhaps he envisioned himself writing destructive viruses as part of a covert weapons project for one of them. "Aren't there any other agencies which would be more interested in what I'm doing?" Priest asked the agents. He didn't get an answer.

Eventually, the Secret Servicemen went away with a Priest-autographed printout of the source code to Satan Bug.

Programming Satan Bug had turned out to be richly rewarding for Priest. Not only had it gotten him recognized immediately in the computer underground, it had made him feared in the trenches of corporate America to the point where the Secret Service had felt compelled to intervene.

Since the Satan Bug panic was a golden opportunity for anti-virus vendors to once again market wares, the stories in the computing press kept coming. *LAN Times* put the virus on the front page of its November 1 issue with the headline, "Be on the Lookout for the Diabolical 'Satan Bug' Virus."[2] *LAN Times* East Coast bureau chief Laura Didio wrote "the Satan Bug is designed to circumvent the security facilities in Novell Inc. Netware's NETX program, thereby allowing it to spread across networks." While Satan Bug may have certainly spread across networks, it had nothing to do with the virus's design. It seemed no matter the truth about Satan Bug, the story just got more pumped up with phlogiston and air as it rolled along.

"What's NETX?" asked Priest when he heard about the *LAN Times* article.

---

2 Laura Didio, "Be on the lookout for the diabolical 'Satan Bug' virus", *LAN Times*, November 1, 1993.

Of course, the *LAN Times* article accurately served as an advertisement for the Satan Bug-detecting software of Norman Data Defense Systems and McAfee Associates. Priest, meanwhile, continued to work on viruses. He had just completed Natas, which he'd turned over to the Secret Service and to phalcon/SKISM for publication in an issue of *40 Hex*. He also uploaded the virus to a couple of bulletin board systems in Southern California. And he finished a very small, 96-byte COM program-infecting virus. And there were other things he was working on, he said.

The most interesting fallout from the Secret Service visit was a job offer from David Stang at Norman Data Defense Systems, said Priest. The virus writer said Stang wanted him to come work for the security expert's company, starting in the summer of 1994, after the hacker finished high school.

Priest said Stang was interested in his opinion about the use of virus code in anti-virus software. Such code wasn't copyrighted, so it was fair game. Priest thought this was a bad idea. Too much virus code, in his opinion, was crappy anyway, so why would anyone want to use it? But Priest said he would think about the job offer.

By May 1994, Priest's Natas virus had cropped up in Mexico City, where, according to one anti-virus software developer, it had been spread by a consultant providing anti-virus software services. Through ignorance and incompetence, the consultant had gotten Natas attached to a copy of the anti-virus software he was using. However, like most of Priest's viruses, Natas was a bit more than most software could handle. The software detected Natas in programs but not in an area of the hard disk known as the master boot record, where the virus also hid itself. The result was tragicomic. The consultant would search computers for viruses. The software would find Natas! Golly, the consultant would think, "Natas is here! I better check other computers, too." And so, the consultant would take his Natas-infected software to other computers where, quite naturally, it would also detect Natas as it spread the virus to the master boot record, a part of the computer where the software could not detect Priest's program.

Natas had come to Mexico from Southern California. The consultant often frequented a virus exchange bulletin board system in Santa Clarita which not only stocked Natas, but also the issue of

40 Hex that contained its source code. He had downloaded the virus, perhaps not fully understood what he was dealing with, and a month or so later uploaded a desperate plea for help with Priest's out-of-control program. You could tell from the date on the cry for help—May 1994—when Natas began being a real problem in Mexico.

Here's the help notice:

```
If you have information on [Natas] please leave
a message here or if you wish ... you can give
us a call . . . and leave us a message in a
file at Antivirus library with information re-
garding where have you seen Natas. For example:
country, state, city, suburb, building (size),
office enviroment (bank,industry,size),
commercial chain, size of machine, net (novell,
lantstic, etc), workstation, etc., (lab?).

Please, Names only of cities or at the most sub-
urbs where infection of NATAS was or has been
detected, will be very much appreciated, so we
can be able to trace the little critter. We
will give similar information of infections on
this country.

Regards!
```

Natas was another typical tricky Priest program. When in computer memory, it masked itself in infected programs and made them appear uninfected. It would also retrieve a copy of the uninfected master boot record it carried encrypted in its body and fake out the user by showing it to him if he tried to go looking for it there. Natas also infected diskettes and spread quickly to programs when they were viewed, copied or looked at by anti-virus software. It was fair to say that computer services providers wielding anti-virus software in a casual manner ought not to have been allowed anywhere near Natas.

Back in San Diego, Priest said he was still being interviewed on the telephone by David Stang and other associates at Norman Data Defense Systems. They were concerned that Priest might leak proprietary secrets to competitors after hiring, so it was a must that he be absolutely sure of the seriousness of his potential employment.

By the end of the interview, Priest thought he didn't have much of a chance at the job, but by July he'd accepted an offer and moved to Fairfax to begin working for David Stang. This was the same David Stang who had written in the July 1992 issue of his *Virus News and Reviews* magazine, "In this office, we try to see things in terms of black and white, rather than gray . . . The problem is that good guys don't wear white hats. Among virus researchers are a large number of seemingly gray individuals . . . This grayness is clear to users. Last week, I asked my class if anyone in the room trusted anti-virus vendors. Not one would raise their hand . . . "

But what did Priest say he was working on at Norman Data Defense Systems?

"A cure for Natas," he laughed softly one afternoon in late July, 1994, in the Norman Data office. Looking over the virus once more, Priest sardonically concluded that his disinfector made it clear the hacker had made Natas a little too easy to remove from infected systems. Apparently, Norman Data Defense had clients in Mexico and at the Secret Service.

You had to admire the moxie of the young American virus programmer. He'd set out in 1992 to emulate the world's greatest virus programmer, Dark Avenger, and ended up being paid cash money to cure the paintpots of computer poison he'd created. As for that poor stone fool, the Dark Avenger, he never even got a handful of chewing gum for his viruses, having the misfortune to have been born in the wrong place, Bulgaria, at the wrong time, during the fall of Communism.

But by the end of the summer, the blush was off the rose for Priest and Norman Data, too. Another manager in the office, Sylvia Moon, didn't like the idea of the hacker working for the company, Priest said. And when management representatives arrived from the parent corporate installation in Norway on an inspection tour and were appraised of Priest's status at a meeting, the hacker heard, they were not pleasantly surprised to learn there was a virus-writer on the staff. Officially, said Priest, there was no reaction, but in reality, the hacker felt, the atmosphere was deeply strained. Nevertheless, said Priest, David Stang maintained that he would protect the hacker's position. And Jack Lewis, said Priest, had contacted the company to set up a luncheon date with the hacker to discuss more technical issues. However, Priest said, David Stang wanted Lewis to provide a Secret Service statement to the effect that the hiring of the hacker wasn't such a bad idea. The luncheon fell through. The Secret Service would provide no such statement because, said Priest, it might be construed as a "conflict of interest."

It all came to an end when one of Priest's acquaintances from the BBSes called the Norman Data office and left a message for "James Priest." Priest was immediately let go. David Stang, said Priest, told him the call was an indication that the hacker couldn't be trusted, that he was still in touch with the underground.

Paranoia and recriminations flew. There had been an intern from William & Mary working at the company whose father was a Pentagon official, said Priest. The rumor was that Priest had been pumping the intern for information on how to penetrate Pentagon computers and siphoning it back into the underground. It was nonsense, said the hacker, but it became the official version of events. These were pretexts, thought Priest. The real reason he had to be shown the door, he said, was pressure from the higher-ups in Norway. They had been presented with him as a done-deal hire and it hadn't set well, he said. David Stang, said Priest, needed a reason to cut him loose and the phone call from a friend had been the peg to hang it on. Priest was a hot potato and he had to go.

Back in San Diego once again, Priest almost sounded relieved. He had a Sylvia Moon-autographed copy of a computer book as a memento from the company and that was it. However, he had finally been able to videotape *The Satan Bug* telemovie. He shifted the VCR into replay and turned to look at his computer while it was playing. But the hacker said he still didn't know what the movie was about when it was over. He had been too busy at the PC to pay attention. Working. . . .

Chain of Fools:
The Underground

Benjamin Franklin once said:

". . . very fond we were of Argument, and very desirous of
confuting each other. Which disputacious Turn, by the way,
is apt to become a very bad Habit, making People often
extreamly disagreeable in Company . . . and thence, besides
souring and spoiling the Conversation, is productive of Disgusts and perhaps Enmities where you may have occasion for
Friendship."

In many respects, you could not coin a better description of certain
regions of cyberspace. And there was no other place in 1994
possessed of more "Disgusts" and "Enmities" than the virus underground in North America.

The NuKE virus-writing group had almost disintegrated. It had
never been much of a group to begin with, and when Nowhere Man
became less and less interested in viruses, one of its last level-
headed members was gone.

The only key players remaining were John Buchanan at the
Black Axis and Rock Steady at Cybernetic Violence. They hated
each other. Everyone else was window-dressing.

Rock Steady, said Nowhere Man, was a terrible judge of
character. He had padded the group with a number of fringe
members who seemed to be either irrational, overly argumentative

or mentally ill. Buchanan was argumentative; Screaming Radish, a virus writer from Melbourne, Australia, seemed both irrational and overtly crazy. For a short period of time, NuKE had included a woman named Typhoid Mary, whom Buchanan became convinced was some kind of deepcover spy from a National Security Agency-financed operation run out of Los Alamos National Laboratory. Nowhere Man had no idea how or why she had gotten into NuKE, but his one conversation with her left him feeling that she was operating with a few cards short of a full deck. Far from being an undercover operative, I thought, Typhoid Mary appeared to be just an employee at the national lab in Los Alamos, who appeared to have an interest in viruses. And her membership in NuKE brought her little but trouble—abuse from Buchanan and excommunication from hobbyist computer networks when more conservative members found she was part of a virus-writing group.

None of this had anything to do with computer viruses, per se, but it's important to relate because it illustrates the fallacy of the picture painted by anti-virus software developers and the media: that the virus underground was a kind of monolithic enemy of society, fighting the men in white hats in a high-tech death struggle for the future of computing. If anything, the virus underground engaged in high-tech death struggles only with itself.

One of these concerned the theory that John Buchanan was a government informer out to provide evidence that would result in jail time for those apprehended. But the conspiracy theorists had mysteriously forgotten that Buchanan had sold cyber-truckloads of viruses to any and all takers and that it was highly unlikely that any such person would be the linchpin of a gigantic sting operation aimed at a the computer underground. Nevertheless, paranoia was the rule of the day for NuKE, so much so, that Screaming Radish finally came completely unglued and engaged in a series of wallet-draining and mystifying phone calls from Australia to myself, Kim Clancy and the Secret Service in an attempt to find out if Buchanan was a "narc."

"Tell your readers this is one Australian who doesn't own a big knife," he said, in apparent reference to his perception that all Americans thought of Australians as junior-league knock-offs of Crocodile Dundee.

Screaming Radish bent my ear for three hours, talking and talking and talking about how Aristotle was "a narc" and how virus writers should receive a percentage of anti-virus software company profits because it was by their actions that consumer products were improved. To prove the point, Screaming Radish had distributed a small program to the NuKE-net virus exchanges which reverse-engineered McAfee Associates' anti-virus scanner and displayed all the virus names it detected along with the corresponding strings of bytes that the program used to identify each virus it was designed to detect. Radish's program really was a nice piece of work if you were interested in such things, and he insisted that by looking over McAfee's scan strings, you could see, in his opinion, how ill-chosen they were, thereby becoming a better consumer of anti-virus software. That no one would use the program for this purpose was beside the point. Screaming Radish really didn't seem to believe that other virus writers would use it as a tool to see what strings of bytes the McAfee software was detecting and quickly alter existing viruses into trivial variants that could no longer be scanned, although that was its obvious use.

Without virus writers, Screaming Radish maintained, the computing public would actually be victimized by even more viruses because there would be no evolutionary pressure on the various software packages to improve and evolve. His program that snatched the virus scan strings from McAfee software was part of this grand plan.

I asked Screaming Radish, who had been a member of the small Australian virus writing group called Southern Corrupted Programming before joining NuKE, what he did besides write viruses and reverse-engineer anti-virus software. He was in his mid-thirties, he said, with a wife, kids and a house. The hacker said he programed Windows applications for good money but "[liked] to keep my hobby separate from my profession. That's a good idea, don't you think?"

Screaming Radish then called Kim Clancy at Bureau of the Public Debt and proceeded to grill her about whether she thought John Buchanan was an informer for the Secret Service. He asked her for a telephone number so he could call the Secret Service directly and ask about Buchanan. Clancy laughed, recalling the hacker's mania. Who knew what was in his head when he decided to call the Secret Service from Australia and sunnily ask to check its list of informants?

Clancy humored Screaming Radish and sent him on his way armed with a Secret Service telephone number.

Back on the NuKE-net in June of 1994, virus writers were congratulating each other over their imaginary war with the anti-virus industry. One hacker, named Sploozo, claimed:

```
On the programming front, the A-V'ers have
constantly been on the defensive — they've
always had to react to what the [virus
programmers] write. Their biggest weapon -
scan strings - won't save you if you're
infected by a brand-new virus. Without scan
strings, what are they left with then . . .

Where they are winning, however, is on the
legislative front. They've successfully forced
the Bureau of Public Debt to remove
hack/phreak/virus files from its BBS recently.
CARO's busy lobbying to make viruses illegal in
the US, Al Solomon's busy going after Apache
Warrior and ARCV over in England . . . The only
thing that the [virus writers] have to defend
themselves—in the US only—is the Bill of Rights.
```

. . . which sounded reasonable until you realized the virus writers on the NuKE-net had so hermetically isolated themselves that they truly had no idea what was going on in the outside world or that the Apache Warrior/ARCV case was two years old and quite dead. By then, New Scotland Yard's computer crime unit was being pushed by Alan Solomon to arrest a new virus writer known as Black Baron, an event that would take the virus underground completely by surprise two weeks later.

Evil Avatar, a hacker who had written the Binary Acid virus, commiserated with Sploozo.

```
It is sad that the public is still ignorant
about the subject because of the self-
proclaimed good guys. The AV's are making the
money and keeping the public
ignorant. What utter rot! They are the bad
guys, not us . . . Perhaps [the US government]
should go after the real criminals - the AV!
```

By 1994, the virus writers who publicly went about their business on the international networks were little more than a menacing-sounding, trivial gang of wishful thinkers. While they pretended to collaborate, they really didn't. The most that could be said was that they traded computer viruses and electronic mail. None of them had even figured out that Priest had gone to work for an anti-virus company.

But it just got crazier. John Buchanan, deviled by another young, impressionable member of NuKE named Firecracker, telephoned his nattering critics in the underground and filled their heads with conflated fictions about evil hackers and the theft of nuclear secrets. Staring at their glowing computer monitors for too long, they believed him.

In mid-June 1994, Firecracker called me up and demanded to know what Buchanan was up to! He said Buchanan had admitted to him that he was part of a secret intelligence operation run by a shadowy branch of the government. The aim was to spy on virus writers and other hackers on the Internet. There was going to be a document shredding party the next working day; those files not shredded were being classified and sealed at the highest level. Someone had just been jailed, and another hacker who'd wandered onto a military Internet site and gotten too close to plans for the movement and reprocessing of weapons-grade plutonium had been scragged. And, Firecracker continued, it was quite probable that Buchanan had also been behind the jailing of Paskell "Geno" Paris. Firecracker was sure he had it all figured out.

Frank Tirado, a computer security specialist at the United States Department of Agriculture who was familiar with the virus underground, said it was his opinion that some of the crazier ideas were started by people "who had no life." As for the number of virus exchange bulletin board systems, tracking them had become meaningless. For two years, John Buchanan had sold viruses to corporate clients and hobbyists who'd contacted him on the FIDO-net. Kids, would-be virus writers and the determined who'd called the Black Axis and been willing to spend for the long distance time had gotten them over the wire for free. A score of other systems had similar policies and with insta-packs of viruses in hand, anyone could start a virus exchange. It had gotten so twisted, the viruses didn't matter, just the numbers. If you could say you had 2,000 or more of them on-line you were a big deal. It didn't matter if you had only the vaguest idea what a computer virus was, had never seen one in action, or if 50 to 75 percent of your files were duplicates, minor hacks of older viruses or non-working junk. It was only the numbers that were important, the numbers which allowed anyone who had read too many of William Gibson's cyberpunk novels to amass these on-line stockpiles of worthless ware.

Orange County in Southern California had its West Coast Institute of Virus Research. Falcon was its sysop and he wanted the system to have the most viruses in the world, a rather grandiose claim even by virus exchange standards.

Orange County is considered a strange place even by Southern California standards. It has no shortage of kooks and reactionaries. For example, it is the home of mad-dog Republican congressman Bob Dornan, the subject of a book called *Shut Up, Fag!* which was written as a sarcastic putdown of his collected wit and wisdom. And the West Coast Institute of Virus Research wasn't Orange County's only big virus exchange. Another was named Digital Decay. In addition to viruses, DD served as a publishing base for another electronic magazine, *Death & Anarchy*, which included interviews with people from the computer underground, virus information and articles on housebreaking and theft of various types of merchandise. *Death & Anarchy* sounded threatening, but you had to keep in mind that the foaming-at-the-mouth style went with the territory of electronic publications in the underground and should not be taken too seriously. It made for exciting reading, though, right alongside *Shut Up, Fag!*

In Arcadia in Southern California's San Gabriel Valley, there was City of Illusion, run by two high school- age sysops who'd read Steven Levy's book *Hackers* and every issue of the cyber-culture magazine, *Mondo 2000.* They were trying to carve out their own piece of the information superhighway and had little understanding about any of the technicalities of computer viruses. Like many others their age, they had just gone out into cyberspace and snatched up every last file labelled as an IBM computer virus that they could find. With a high-speed modem it was an easy job in late 1993. City of Illusion came to an abrupt end when one of the sysops was apprehended by police while trying to steal a pay phone. His parents thought it was time to put the bulletin board on permanent hold. And there was Micro Information Systems Services in the

Antelope Valley, just north of Los Angeles, the last stop for Priest's Natas virus before it went on to roost in Mexico City.

Any one of these systems—or countless others like them across the country—would have been enough to curl John Dvorak's hair in 1991 had he known of them. His book on PC telecommunications made much of Hell Pit,[1] but, virus-wise, the system was far from unique anymore.

As for Hell Pit, it had purged its user base and gone private. In an introductory screen to the system, Nowhere Man explained that if the information highway was going to be anything like the sunny, exaggerated visions predicted by the media, no one at Hell Pit wanted any part of it. It was a satirical rant which summed up what much of the on-line community had degenerated into during the great info-highway hype of 1994:

```
    . . . Our file bases are not filled with fifty
different CD-ROM [shareware] collections . . .
Our sysop is not a lifeless, forty-something
wash-up whose sole interest is adding more
nodes and doors to his pathetic system . . .
When you call the Hell Pit you are not
confronted by a bunch of thirteen-year-old
geeks who spend their day 'chatting' with
similar losers with no friends . . . Here you
are never harassed by someone or something
named 'BalFrikBot' who likes to message you 30k
files about applesauce, nor [interrupted] every
thirty seconds by some inane college student
from Zimbabwe who gets his jollies from posing
as other people and changing the [conversation]
base topic to 'CHeETOZ!!!!!' We don't flood
your terminal with . . . fake mail from your
account to [the Usenet's] alt.sex.ferrets . . .
Messages posted on this system do not contain .
. . [coded] copies of the Encyclopedia
Britannica - split into [bite-size] chunks for
your convenience, of course . . . We do not
```

---

1 John Dvorak & Nick Anis, *John Dvorak's Guide to PC Telecommunications, 2nd. Ed.*, McGraw Hill, 1992.

carry MUDs, MUCKs, MUSEs, or other [Dungeons &
Dragons-type] resource-wasting games. We
restrict our access: Billy Idol, Adam Curry,
Wil Wheaton, and Al Gore will *NEVER* have
accounts here. We are not another vertebra in
the homogeneous National Science Foundation
Internet backbone. We do not trade Visa cards,
PBX codes, [voice mail box] accounts, or loop
numbers . . . We are not an authorized
'Institute of Virus Research' that is part of a
nationwide franchise system that mirrors a
second-rate virus exchange in Bumblefun, Dixie
. . . We don't attempt to build pipe bombs out
of marshmallows, PVC tubing and Lemon-Fresh Joy
. . . We don't carry [picture files] of alleged
UFO wreckage, distribute instructions on how to
cast magic spells that improve your
intelligence, sex life, and cholesterol level,
or stock strange right-wing conspiracy tracts
with racist overtones. We are NOT a Fed board
. . . We do not run Windows. We do not
subscribe to Prodigy, America On-Line, Compuserve, ImagiNation, the WELL, or MindVox. We
do not buy '...For Dummies' books . . . We are
the Hell Pit and we are sick of what our world
is turning into. We are one of the few
bastions of sanity and reliable information in
this increasingly incompetent, commercialized,
crowded, 'user-friendly' world . . ."

Far better to lock the door and install a secret password now,
Hell Pit was saying, than allow the kind of callers who would
overrun the system with nutty conspiracy theories, flame wars and
mountains of files with all the worth of one-page recipes for
transmuting lead into gold.

Not everyone in the virus underground or on-line was erratic
or a relentless shill, though. In Texas, there was Stormbringer, a
sober-minded hacker who took seriously Fred Cohen's theories on
productive computer viruses—replicating software automatons
which could be trusted with various functions on the computer of
the future.

Stormbringer never bought the popular conception of the computer virus: that of a program designed to be purely destructive, ready to trash a home or corporate personal computer at a moment's notice. He could be thought of as the complete opposite of Priest, although he held an admiration for the San Diego hacker's technical skill.

In 1993 Stormbringer won a $100 cash prize in Mark Ludwig's First International Virus Writing Contest. Notices of it had been spread on the Internet, with the predictable cries of indignation and personal outrage from virus researchers like pompous Vesselin Bontchev.

"Freedom of expression is a wonderful right, but Ludwig should be aware that the U.S. constitution does not apply to the whole Universe and thus, some things allowed by it might be illegal in some other countries," wrote Bontchev in an April 1994 issue of *Computer underground Digest.* "Therefore, anybody who decides to participate Mr. Ludwig's contest, is strongly advised to consult a local lawyer. Of course, it would be much better to ponder a bit how unethical the whole thing is and to refuse to participate the contest at all . . . Maybe this is because Ludwig understands that those people might be held legally responsible in some countries for such activities? In this case, his contest is nothing more than an incitement to commit a crime . . . "

The object of Ludwig's contest had been to write the smallest possible virus capable of infecting a program while still preserving the functionality of the host. This was the contest that Priest had dithered around about entering with his 96-byte virus. Stormbringer's entry was the winner at 101 bytes. It was still a mere digital dot.

"I think viruses are starting to push into the realm of artificial life—they're not there yet, but it's the best we've got," Stormbringer said in an interview for the *Los Angeles Reader* in early 1994.[2] "I think it's a legitimate research field and would hate to see it squelched before it produced any real fruit.

---

2 George Smith, "User-friendly viruses: They'll keep your files private . . . and the Feds don't like that", *Los Angeles Reader*, February 4, 1994.

"All censorship of viruses will do is restrict the knowledge from people that are likely to end up on the receiving end of a virus—people that might otherwise be able to deal with viruses if they could find out how they worked," he continued. "I mean, think about it. Do you want your government telling you what you can or cannot learn?"

Although the concept of computer viruses as examples of artificial life was almost completely fanciful, Stormbringer kept ruminating over the idea of a productive virus and by July 1994 had written a program he called "Good Virus 1.01." "Good Virus 1.01" was modelled on a hot topic on the Internet—free, strong encryption.

Mark Ludwig had distributed a boot sector virus called Potassium Hydroxide, or KOH—the compound's chemical formula — in late 1993 which was also designed to be a "good virus." KOH was meant to be installed on any IBM-clone personal computer where it would, on command, encrypt everything stored in the machine and any floppy diskette, in essence providing a formidable digital lock which could be opened only by the person who knew the password. Operating in the background, the virus was the first thing to wake up when the computer was turned on. It asked for the password and then went about encrypting and decrypting everything on the machine throughout the day, invisibly. However, if anyone tried to get at the machine when the user was away, the virus became a wall, making everything on the machine unusable electronic garbage.

Stormbringer's "Good Virus 1.01" was a less complex interpretation of the KOH concept. It was a program-infecting virus that came with a pop-up menu called by a keystroke. When you installed the virus, it didn't do anything but remain in memory, waiting for instructions. It could be commanded to infect specific programs and also to remove itself from them by checking the appropriate selections in its menu box. It also could encrypt and decrypt selected data on command using different passwords. Stormbringer had written it to be used in highly bureaucratic environments where someone might feel their computer and files were being snooped upon. "Good Virus 1.01," since it wasn't an orthodox program, was easy to hide on a system. It could parasitize other programs just like a standard program-infecting virus and it could also be used to quickly lock up sensitive information.

Around the same time, Stormbringer produced a disinfection program for the viruses which had been discovered in the United Kingdom and made their author, the Black Baron, the target of another ARCV-like anti-virus company-inspired manhunt.

But the virus underground wasn't the only place that could be criticized for being sprinkled with citizens who seemed patently nuts. The actions of the computer virus industry and the American market were equally contrived and cracked.

Chain of Fools:
The Suits

In 1994 it was safe to say that from a retail standpoint, American consumers had the worst anti-virus software in the world to choose from. Symantec had busied itself acquiring its rivals like Fifth Generation Systems, Certus and Central Point Software, an anti-competitive strategy which was a detriment to the industry and users in general. Fifth Generation had licensed a product called Untouchable from an Israeli firm known as BRM. The product was superior to Symantec's Norton Anti-virus in almost every way, but its American distribution was killed.

Through 1992 and 1993 the Ziff-Davis publications *PC Magazine* and *PC Computing* held anti-virus software evaluations that gave editor's choice awards to Central Point Anti-Virus and high marks to Norton Anti-Virus, the two software packages which virus writers and experts on viruses knew were the worst.

"The features and performance of Central Point Anti-virus for DOS and Windows are impressive," wrote *PC Magazine* in March 1993.[1] "No wonder a stripped-down version of the program was chosen to be included in [Microsoft's] DOS 6.0."

---

1 Ribin Raskin with M. E. Kabay, "Keeping up your guard: One year after the great Michelangelo scare, viruses, virus creation tools, and antivirus software have gotten smarter and more powerful", *PC Magazine*, March 16, 1993.

Impressively bad was a more accurate assessment. The magazine rated the software "excellent" at simple virus detection. The magazine arrived at this conclusion after pitting the software against eleven different viruses. But later the same year, a European computer publication called *Personal Computer Magazine* reported that Central Point Anti-virus wouldn't even perform reliably enough to be tested against a collection of viruses which numbered in the thousands.[2]

The latter types of results were backed up again and again by sources as separate as virus writers, Mark Ludwig and virus researchers who communicated on the Internet, but did not appear in the pages of Ziff-Davis magazines.

The editors at *PC Magazine* thought they could accurately appraise anti-virus software packages in a handful of paragraphs, using a handful of free-lancers and a handful of viruses. One of their main criteria for anti-virus excellence appeared to be packaging and user interface of the program in question. It seemed to be the reporters' reasoning that American consumers would use only software that looked nice, and if it didn't look nice but was excellent in function it would never get off the shelf, so far better to have crummy anti-virus software that looked nice and actually was used, than none at all. Central Point Anti-virus did look good on your screen but the free-lance reporters made no allowance for the fact that appearance is often just a matter of personal taste; some of the other packages looked nice too, and worked better, but unfortunately, their poor fool programmers apparently didn't use the color scheme which the writers at *PC Magazine* had determined American consumers wanted.

The simple explanation for this anti-intuitive type of magazine-mandated consumer ripoff was that Ziff-Davis and similar publications existed only as toadies to the software and hardware mainstays of the computer industry and they were extremely sensitive to advertising revenues. Central Point Software and Symantec spent good money for ads in glossy computer magazines; many of the other anti-virus software developers didn't. The Ziff-Davis magazines generally featured carefully chosen sets of columnists

---

2 *Virus Bulletin*, January, 1994, p. 14.

fond of dressing in power suits and appearing in phony-looking, sepia-toned photographs. Superficially, they looked impressive, but on closer inspection a reader would find that when these experts were not writing self-congratulatory, speculative thumbsuckers on what was going to be hot or trendy in six months, they generally took on only straw men of their own creation—easy targets incapable of defending themselves, or industry scandals which were already common knowledge. It was a lead pipe cinch none of them were the kind of journalists to use their bully pulpits as platforms to denounce popular advertisers. And it was a good bet that most of what they knew about anti-virus software and computer viruses could be gained from vendor press releases. In short, they were courtiers to the rich and famous in the microcomputer industry.

The virus underground had absolutely nothing to do with the lack of quality retail anti-virus software in the United States, although its members were good at pointing it out. The bad software was purely a function of business decisions and editorial actions taken with no consideration for consumers. Central Point had licensed its program from an Israeli firm called Carmel Software long before the virus underground was even a gleam in John Buchanan's eye in the United States. Any faults the software had came from Carmel and wound up being passed on to Microsoft when Bill Gates or one of his flunkies made a decision to license a slightly less functional copy of it for bundling with Microsoft's DOS 6.0.

It was fortunate for PC users that John McAfee's shareware distribution scheme for SCAN was so successful at penetrating corporate markets, for while the program had some faults, it was leagues superior to the competition at Symantec and Central Point.

In mid-1993, the vendor spoke out against the decision to pass on to MS-DOS 6.0's users a watered-down edition of Central Point's already shaky program. It was junk, a McAfee Associates press release implied, and it would not be a good substitute for the firm's own virus-fighting programs.

"Based on initial responses from its customers, which include 66 of the Fortune 100 companies, McAfee concluded that the virus protection found in MS-DOS 6.0 is not a solution for corporate virus protection," ran the press release.[3]

McAfee continued by stating the new set of utilities in MS-DOS 6.0 failed to deliver features or benefits comparable to those of independent utilities. "In particular, Microsoft will have a difficult time matching the level of technical expertise and customer service for anti-virus software that is currently offered by McAfee Associates.

".... Central Point Software, the company that provided the virus protection software for DOS 6.0, has a 61-percent virus detection rate for the most recent version of its anti-virus product, according to an independent certification done in March 1993 against 1,956 viruses. This compares to a 96-percent detection rate for McAfee's virus protection software, according to the same certification."

Much of the press release was standard corporate boilerplate and John McAfee might be criticized for being a sour grape, were it not for the fact that others not connected with McAfee Associates were saying the same thing. Central Point Anti-virus had proven extremely vulnerable to a variety of standard virus techniques, including polymorphism. Mark Ludwig had demonstrated that the Microsoft version, in addition to being a slow performer, simply crashed when it ran across elementary variants of Mutation Engine viruses.[4] It was not even particularly effective at detecting minor hacks of common viruses like Jerusalem. Ludwig attributed the program's success in the marketplace to its colorful appearance, laconically commenting that the industry was into providing a "warm and fuzzy" feeling to consumers who liked graphics and other smoke and mirrors on their computer screen.

Virus writers had also targeted the program as standard operating procedure. Priest's Satan Bug neutralized code that Central Point Anti-virus added to programs to "immunize" them, although in fairness, it must be noted that his virus had special tricks to get around McAfee software, too.

A part of Central Point Anti-virus, and by extension the Microsoft version, was designed to remain in computer memory as a sentry against virus action. It proved deceptively simple to bypass. Less than ten bytes of code could be added to any virus in order to

---

3 George Smith, "Wampeter, foma and granfalloons: McAfee Associates waste little time getting around to criticizing Microsoft Anti-virus", *Crypt Newsletter*, No. 14, March, 1993.

4 *Computer Virus Developments Quarterly*, Vol 1., No 3., Spring, 1993, p. 3.

fake a user request from the keyboard for the sentry to remove itself from duty in computer memory. By mid-1994, so many viruses included this as a standard feature, just like a car's seat belts, that researchers and virus writers stopped mentioning it as remarkable. Central Point Anti-virus had been an easy target, and virus writers quickly moved on to other software. Ironically, you could tell by the degree of their interest what was a competent product. The hands-down winner, in this regard, was Frans Veldman's Thunderbyte software. In an effort to make an end run around the growing numbers of viruses —which required constant scan string updating —Veldman had made his anti-virus scanner extremely sensitive to subsets of code which tended to be generic to computer viruses, but not legitimate programs. Fridrik Skulason had also factored this feature into his software, but did not emphasize it to the high degree that Veldman did.

The feature was called "heuristic" detection and it could be used to examine programs for evidence of as-yet-unknown viruses. For the increasing number of run-of-the-mill virus specimens cranked out by virus toolkits, it was more than adequate.

For example, Veldman's Thunderbyte scanner would look for what was called a suspicious jump construct in the inspected program. Almost all file viruses had to manipulate the beginning of a host program with instructions which would tell the computer to jump to the virus code, usually added to the end of the infected program, so the virus could take control and do whatever it had been programed to before handing control back to the target program.

One common type of program, known as a .COM executable, demanded that most viruses which attached themselves to the end of it insert a jump instruction, or "jmp," at the beginning of the file.

If the virus code contained jumps to other routines of instructions immediately after the beginning of the rest of the virus, now stowed at the end of the infected program, Veldman's software issued a warning.

In general, the code often followed this pattern:

```
jmp TO_VIRUS   ;beginning of infected host
                  ;host code
                  ;host code
_____

TO_VIRUS:          ;virus added to end of
host
                  ;starts here
jmp SKIP
                  ;more virus code
                  ;more virus code
SKIP:
_____
```

The Thunderbyte software looked for other constructs and strings of generic virus-like computer code, weighed the number of warnings they generated and made an educated guess about whether the program was infected with an unknown virus. The user could feather the sensitivity of Veldman's program or allow it to be determined automatically. It was a useful tool, but required some knowledge on the part of a user and the realization that other perfectly legitimate programs were bound to set off virus-like code alarms. For some system administrators faced with scanning thousands of networked PCs, the feature was merely frustrating, as they did not want to be burdened with the additional task of evaluating Thunderbyte's complicated "heuristic" results and the concomitant false alarms.

Virus writers, however, thought the feature was very keen and they marveled over and analyzed it, with the aim of writing viruses which set off as few of Veldman's software alarms as possible.

Thunderbyte was also Priest's special interest. He wrote viruses, like Natas and Jackal, designed to retaliate against Veldman's technology. The second issue of *40 Hex* Hardcopy contained a lengthy product review and analysis of Thunderbyte Anti-virus by another member of phalcon/SKISM, too.

Some overseas anti-virus software developers clearly hated the numbers game which tied their technology to a scanner that had to be constantly updated to retain consumer confidence. Even though the great majority of viruses were never going to show up in the wild, developers had to include them in their software, no matter how trivial, or face flunking any consumer test based on sheer numbers of virus variants. The developers who eschewed the scanner approach based their software on recognition of basic computer virus behavior. They would take a "snapshot" of a system which could be used as a baseline to measure subsequent activity. Computer viruses, by nature, had to make changes in the baseline, and by regularly checking the integrity of the programs, vital areas of the hard disk and computer memory, viruses could be trapped and removed. The knocks the scanner-pushers leveled against this approach were that it asked the user to actually wait for a virus to act, interpretation of results was difficult, and reloading large numbers of virus-contaminated files was time-consuming in the event of a fast-spreading major infection. It was also more difficult to sell to Americans, who could be more easily persuaded that anti-virus scanning was a kind of magic bullet cure for computer viruses.

The criticisms had some value, but in the face of greater and greater numbers of viruses, scanners didn't seem such a hot answer, either.

The most sophisticated example from the alternative thinkers was a set of programs called Invircible, marketed from Israel. Invircible's author, Zvi Netiv, felt that it was possible to store approximately seventy bytes from the beginning, or header, of every program on a computer's hard disk without imposing a significant overhead on system resources. Once the system had been secured by the Invircible software, an unknown virus could be removed reliably from large numbers of infected programs by properly restoring the header, wiping the virus off the beginning or end of the file it had attached itself to, and properly rearranging other factors critical to the programs which the virus might have deranged when on the system.

Invircible was designed to function in the teeth of stealthy virus infection and return results which quickly uncovered new viruses by identifying their action in memory and trapping them in a series of clever virus-baits launched as decoys. Netiv knew Invircible wasn't as much of a no-brainer as firing up one anti-virus scanner and forgetting everything else, but he was convinced it was the only sensible approach for the future. But, since all of the product testing performed by magazines and researchers like Vesselin Bontchev was suborned to the idea of the supremacy of the anti-virus scanner, Netiv's programs were often overlooked, as was anyone who decided to hoe the same row. The scanner horn had been tooted so loudly for many years, developers and researchers had a vested career interest in continuing to support it or see many of their ideas about computer virus control get thrown into the dumper and their reputation as experts dissolve in obsolescence. John Buchanan certainly recognized that the anti-virus industry's absorption with scanners could be exploited to crazy degrees. He had written the Aristo-Hack to produce as many junk viruses as possible. In July 1994 he finished what he called the Metric Butt-load of Code Producer, or MBCP, which again used the phalcon/SKISM virus toolkit to mass produce hundreds of viruses, each of which had slightly differing, insignificant variables, creating a host of essentially identical viruses differing by from one to about fifty bytes. On the face of it, such a development wouldn't seem to matter until you looked inside one of the anti-virus scanners and saw that the better ones already included scan strings for at least thirty viruses produced by the phalcon/SKISM toolkit. And, indeed, it would not have mattered, had the anti-virus software developers only been concerned with generically detecting such viruses. However, they had all been sucked into exact identification so that precise virus removal routines could be adopted in their software. This meant, no matter how trivial the virus, developers would be duty bound to analyze it and include removal capability in their software. It was a goal that ensured a Sisyphean amount of labor, since even the smallest mistake in virus identification would result in a ruined file when software was called to disinfect a program.

So, Buchanan's idea was to use the Metric Butt-load of Code Producer to ensure a continuing flow of a hundred or so virus packets, with each virus numbered serially, which could be used for two purposes: 1) to plague anti-virus software developers with endless amounts of busy work; and (2) to pollute rival virus exchanges with even more junk programs which the sysops would never bother to look at.

To make the job more complicated, Buchanan was using a shareware program created by a Southern California high-school programmer named Jeremy Lilley who had fancied hanging out on virus exchanges. Lilley had devised a program, called PROTEX-COM, which attached an encryption shell to another. The idea was to secure a program of interest from minor attempts at reverse-engineering. Lilley's program, however, was a new twist on the idea.

It used the Dutch virus writer Masud Khafir's Trident Polymorphic Engine to provide a different encryption layer every time it was used. Lilley had been castigated in the underground for using the TPE and not having the good sense to remove the Dutch virus writer's initials from his ripped-off copy of the encryption engine, but Buchanan found a use for the program, anyway. Not only did it put a minor disguise on his usual PS-MPC hacks, it raised the possibility that some would be initially identified as TPE viruses, which were a whole different kettle of fish as far as the anti-virus industry was concerned.

Abandoning scanner technology, or at least downgrading the emphasis on it, would have cut this idiotic Gordian knot, but Buchanan knew this would never occur. Along with everyone else watching the field, it was easy for him to see that as the number of IBM computer viruses arched toward 5,000 by mid-1994, company after company was increasing the frequency of its software updates. Paradoxically, the effectiveness of the products was declining. And competent vendors continued to be driven from the market as software evaluations continued to crown the most non-functional programs as consumer choices. (Central Point Anti-virus's software was again bafflingly dubbed the best by National Software Testing Laboratories in late summer 1994.[5] Although its performance was still poor, if you read between the lines, Central Point's "usability," or pretty interface, was what carried the day.)

John Buchanan was still selling viruses, too. One repeat client was another mysterious German, this time going by the name Hans Peter Boehm.

The anti-virus industry, though, didn't really need John Buchanan's help to create more viruses for the public to worry about. It did fine on its own, generating even more tales of dread "super viruses" in the summer of 1994.

The following case was so absurd, it inspired this joke:

Pete: What's the difference between an anti-virus software vendor and a virus writer?

---

5 "Virus prevention NLSs: Seven convenient and effective programs that defend against the threat of computer viruses", *Byte Magazine*, August, 1994.

Re-Pete: Gee, I dunno, Pete!
Pete: The anti-virus software vendor can afford to staff a
    public relations department.

Although it's easy to see how the quip would be guaranteed to raise
the hackles on conservative elements within the world of computing, it remained quite a mystery why much of the on-line computer
press still reacted like stone idiots when confronted with p.r. touting
super viruses more than two years after Michelangelo.

A small anti-virus company from Brier, Washington, called
Reflex, claimed to have discovered a virus called Junkie on an
unnamed client's system in Ann Arbor, Michigan, in the summer
of 1994. A company press release outlining the find subsequently
landed at the on-line *NewsBytes* news service, which republished
most of the Reflex press release verbatim as news.[6]

"Another Super-Virus Discovered," trumpeted the title of the
June 2 *NewsBytes* article baring the Junkie threat.

NewsBytes proceeded to reprint the advice of Reflex flack Bob
Reed, who claimed, "The only known cure is re-formatting the
[computer's] hard disk." And stupid advice it was. Junkie virus
could—in a pinch—be removed from infected machines without
the use of anti-virus software, and it could certainly be removed
without eliminating all the data on the computer's hard disk. In fact,
the advice attributed to Reflex was so bad it should have raised
questions among computer journalists whether the company even
staffed the kind of experts that should be relied upon when looking
for anti-virus security.

Another representative from Reflex tried to backtrack on the
advice to disinfect Junkie by erasing the data structures on the hard
disk, shifting the blame to Ziff-Davis On-line reporter Doug Vargas
who, the Reflex rep said, told readers "the only way to get rid of
the virus is to format the drive and start over."

"Evidently, this was lost in the translation from the Reflex
engineers to Doug Vargas . . . ," claimed the company spokesman.
In any case, it gave the impression Reflex representatives had no

---

6 "Another super-virus discovered", *Newsbytes*, June 2, 1994.

idea what they were talking about and that on-line reporters weren't helping matters either.

The Reflex reps stressed that the virus utilized alarming new techniques to enhance its virulence. It could, they said, be spread by anti-virus software to every other susceptible program on the computer. This was dutifully passed on by *NewsBytes* and later Compuserve On-line, which repackaged much of the original June 2 *NewsBytes* wirecopy for republication on June 15 as part of its *On-Line Today* news service.

Again this was fallacious, mostly by error of omission. We've seen viruses which were spread by the action of anti-virus programs in earlier chapters. Of course, anti-virus specialists had been well-acquainted with such tricks since at least 1992. Even the cheapest manuals supplied with their software described the mode of action in some detail.

Junkie was also a polymorphic virus, said *NewsBytes*. Crap again.

Bill Arnold, an IBM anti-virus software developer, said, "For what it's worth, [Junkie] is easily detected with scan strings with wildcards . . ."[7] Junkie was not polymorphic. It was encrypted in so basic a manner a unique string of instructions could simply be extracted from the code and immediately folded into existing anti-virus software. At the time, IBM's anti-virus software detected Junkie, as did a number of other competing programs. However, Compuserve attributed to Frank Horowitz of Reflex another "good salesman's" claim: that anti-virus scanner software couldn't find Junkie, period.

To top it off, Junkie wasn't common. Outside of the alleged report from Ann Arbor, Michigan, the only other claim to surface in the days to follow came from Malmo, a city in Sweden. Junkie was actually more virulent when amplified by the power of journalism. A story on it had even been picked up by *The Times Picayune* newspaper in New Orleans.

"The only known comprehensive method of detection and prevention [for Junkie] at this date is . . . from Reflex," read the

---

7 Public post by IBM's Bill Arnold in Compuserve's National Computer Security Association special interest group, June 16, 1994. Subject: The "Junkie" Virus.

company's press release on the virus. Paradoxically, the press release mentioned the company had to rely on a competitor's product, Frans Veldman's Thunderbyte anti-virus scanner, to help identify the virus—a bit of news noticeably lacking from most on-line stories dealing with Junkie.

The Compuserve news service also attached hearsay on another virus, called SMEG, to the Junkie story. Funneled through Horowitz, SMEG was dubbed another super virus infecting the financial districts of London. Unfortunately, it was just more silly exaggeration. Richard Ford, an Englishman who edited the trade journal *Virus Bulletin*, estimated that only between two and 12 cases of SMEG had been found in the United Kingdom.[8] Of those, only two sightings were rock solid, said Ford, downplaying the news, which had been stirred up by Alan Solomon's S&S International.

Solomon, meanwhile, had again been working behind the scenes, calling John Buchanan for news on the whereabouts of the SMEG viruses' author, Black Baron. Obviously, there was going to be an arrest, just like with ARCV, as soon as Solomon found what he wanted, he implied. Although SMEG had been initially tut-tutted by Ford, the editor of *Virus Bulletin* abruptly changed his position on the urgency of the SMEG virus story when the news of Black Baron's arrest broke, soliciting anyone on the networks to turn information over to New Scotland Yard if they had been attacked by the SMEG viruses.

Ironically, the to-do about SMEG and Junkie got the attention of the underground, which had been completely oblivious to their existence. Although no one in the underground had a sample of the SMEG virus at the beginning of June, due to the publicity, a handful of hackers started making inquiries and by the second week of the month had been able to obtain a working copy of one of the versions of SMEG—there were actually two—by way of our old German friend, Gerhard Maier. Maier had continued to burnish his reputation as a virus trader, and the copy of one of the SMEG programs he supplied came attached to a copy of the MS-DOS text editor. It

---

8 Public post by *Virus Bulletin* editor Richard Ford in Compuserve's National Computer Security Association special interest group, May 26, 1994. Subject: SMEG virus incidence.

was quickly passed around the United States to anyone with the wit to ask via network electronic mail along the FIDO-net backbone and through the Internet service known as Internet Relay Chat. Some refused to take a hit on the Junkie virus press release. A reporter for *Information Week* magazine furnished an article which, in short, called the affair nonsense. Earlier, he had contacted Mark Ludwig, and although the author of *The Little Black Book of Computer Viruses* hadn't seen Junkie, he informed the reporter the case for it was quite probably over-stated.

Perhaps the most interesting facet of the Junkie virus story was the way news concerning it was spread, twisted and manipulated into another frightening tale which created a dumb reality of its own. The fact that Junkie was publicized ensured that although it was rare the day the bozos at Reflex decided to write a press release about the virus in hopes of cadging some extra business, the moment the news hit the virus underground there would be plenty of people who did their best to make reality parallel fiction.

Rod Fewster, Australia's Thunderbyte Anti-virus agent, commented in the weeks following the Junkie brouhaha, "[It] rocketed from nowhere in April and May to become the number four reported virus here in June . . . I don't think it could have accomplished this feat without help."

"It was virtually unknown in the wild until the media gave it 'supervirus' status, then every lamer in the country went looking for a copy and began spreading it," he continued. "Within a week of the media beat-up, fifty-one people [produced] thirty-two different infected samples."

Which, translated, meant: The average denizen of the virus underground generally had no idea about any of the viruses he had his hands on, but as soon as the anti-virus industry stoked the media into making one appear sexy, it would be time to go digging through the net of bulletin boards looking for the file so that it could be passed around or planted on the computers of uncomprehending teachers, students or co-workers.

Junkie was not an intentionally destructive virus, but because it infected floppy disks, the system area of the hard disk and programs so well, it was mildly annoying if your machine was afflicted with it.

As for the SMEG program-infecting viruses, they were destructive. Black Baron, their author, had made them polymorphic

using his Simulated Metamorphic Encryption Generator (SMEG),
which used the now pro forma naming convention for encryption
devices started by the Dark Avenger Mutation Engine (DAME).
The viruses also had the potential to smash the data structures
on the hard disk, at which time they would display the message:

```
Your hard-disk is being corrupted, courtesy of PATHOGEN!
Programmed in the U.K. (Yes, NOT Bulgaria!) [C] The Black Baron
1993-4. Featuring SMEG v0.1: Simulated Metamorphic EnEcryption
Generator! 'Smoke me a kipper, I'll be back for breakfast.....'
Unfortunately some of your data won't!!!!!
```

One of Alan Solomon's agents sounded the alarm on the
networks as the CARO member called up John Buchanan looking
for any information on the whereabouts of Black Baron. It was
obvious this was going down like the Apache Warrior/ARCV
affair. Black Baron was going to be the target of a New Scotland
Yard computer crime unit dragnet with Alan Solomon and S&S
International acting as the unofficial intelligence service.

Graham Cluley, one of S&S International's representatives on
Compuserve, retreated slightly on June 22, 1994, when accused of
over-hyping the SMEG viruses.

"Some of the stuff in the press about SMEG has been distinctly
over-the-top," Cluley conceded. "However, I feel [our] alert . . .
was justified."[9]

"[One] customer of ours found the virus on a BBS, where—it
appears—the virus author had deliberately infected a shareware
anti-virus package," he continued. "We weren't aware of whether
he had uploaded this anti-virus package to any other BBSes, but
there was no reason to believe he had not."

On the July 13, 1994, a man authorities thought was Black
Baron was bagged by British police from the Devon & Cornwall
Constabulary Fraud Squad accompanied by agents from the computer crime unit of New Scotland Yard. The alleged virus writer
was subsequently released on bail.

---

9 Public post by S&S International's Graham Cluley in Compuserve's Nationa
Computer Security Association special interest group, June 22, 1994. Subject:
PATHOGEN/SMEG query.

Alan Solomon and company were not going to stop pursuing their ritualistic attempts to get a virus writer convicted, no matter if the evidence on the threat was soggy or previous efforts had failed. Perhaps by the time you have read this book, they will have succeeded and Black Baron will have made computer crime history in the United Kingdom. Ask about it next year.

And you may have already noticed the double standard within the anti-virus industry concerning virus writers. If not, I'll repeat it again just so you don't forget: Black Baron and destructive, polymorphic viruses equals bad, bad juju. Priest and destructive, polymorphic viruses equals hot property.

Yes, it was a long chain of cheats, hypocrites and fools that stretched from the heart of the anti-virus industry, deep into the virus underground. It was so corrupt, corroded and tangled, no one could be blamed for not wanting to mess with it.

Bellying Up to the Bottom Line

The twenty-seven months between March 1992 and June 1994 had been more than enough time to examine the world of computer viruses, the virus underground and the anti-virus industry. Events had started to repeat themselves. The virus game was the same, it was only the names that changed.

There was the continued production of virus toolkits, mostly modelled after Dark Angel's PS-MPC. None of them caught on, either because they flat out didn't work or their products weren't sufficiently different from the surfeit of virus source code that could now be found on virus exchange bulletin boards to evoke any interest.

Alan Solomon had found another virus writer to make an example of. Maybe this time, his personal *jihad* would bear fruit. However, you couldn't help but suspect that even if the English software developer had poured gasoline over Black Baron, hauled him into Picadilly Circus and set him ablaze at high noon, it wouldn't have made a difference to the virus underground. Simply stated, most of its members would never have looked up from their programming, or whatever it was they were doing, long enough to notice.

After all, no one in the underground had paid any attention to Joseph Popp. Only a few knew Apache Warrior of the Association of Really Cruel Viruses. No one knew Priest had gone into anti-virus work. Take heed from the misfortune of Black Baron? Bet against it.

Conversely, the arrest of Black Baron could be seen as a good anti-virus sales tool. It made for a good pitch to corporate clients. Even a fool could see anyone would feel they were in good hands *vis-à-vis* viruses if they thought the software they were buying was programed by some fellow who had helped jail an infamous virus author! You could almost picture it: Black Baron, the poster boy for S&S International in 1995.

John Buchanan's old NuKE_TheWorld virus writer's echo had finally made it onto the FIDO-net as a legitimate message feed. Now it was called Virus_nfo and was hosted from the Brokedown Palace bulletin board in Newport News/Virginia Beach. Viruses of interest flowed up and down the backbone of the FIDO-net, from satellites to ground receivers. Virus_nfo had its faults, but at least readers didn't have to put up with the constant advertising of the anti-virus shareware peddlers. Even the shareware boosters had lost control of their echos. Sure, the straight virus information echos were moderated and the rules said you couldn't curse or post virus code. But the reality was that virus exchanges and virus writers were so deeply enmeshed within the structure of the network, it was impossible to keep them out. In late July, Deathboy, another NuKE virus writer, posted a trio of simplistic but annoying viruses named Howard Stern, Bad Motherboard and Pumpkinhead into the FIDO virus information echo controlled by Thunderbyte Anti-virus's American representative, Jeff Cook. If Paskell Paris had not been in prison, he would have laughed at the incident. There was little the moderator could do except get angry.

You could always call virus writers nasty names, though, which is what occurred most of the time. Where once the FIDO-net virus information echos had gamely attempted to keep the subject focused on virus control, in 1994 they had degenerated into an electronic free-for-all where the same three or four apparently mentally ill individuals savagely libeled each other, virus code was posted publicly, and the same string of advertisements for anti-virus shareware circulated endlessly.

John Buchanan still occasionally sold his Black Axis virus collection. In the two years he had been doing it, collections had gone to anti-virus software developers, security consultants, hobbyists and other computer professionals. It was quite unsurprising that some of these people put them to uses less lofty than academic. One Black Axis collection had landed in the hands of a computer security administrator from Virginia Beach, stationed on the aircraft carrier George Washington. He had been caught attempting to contaminate computers on the carrier and relieved of his position as a security manager. The Navy hushed the incident up.

Another of Buchanan's collections had been purchased by an employee working at the old Strategic Air Command base in Barksdale, Louisiana. The employee had been caught attempting to plant a virus as the system he'd been working at crashed. Yes, it sure was a twisted world.

Virus collections had also finally made it to CD-ROM. The development came only after people had figured out how to successfully market mind-rotting amounts of shareware and pornography, but it had arrived just the same, despite the incredible negative image of computer viruses. The first compact disk into the market was a volume called *Forbidden Secrets*, manufactured by a company that had accumulated quite a bit of experience selling CD-ROM collections of shareware and "adult" pictures. Mark Ludwig topped it, however, with his *Outlaws from America's Wild West* collection. It was a bonanza of virus files, certainly more than any sane person could want if they weren't intimately involved in computer virus work. It immediately raised the specter of anyone who didn't mind defying Ludwig's license mounting the CD-ROM as a file library attached to their bulletin board, making it possible for anyone with one hundred dollars cash money to make a bid for the title "largest virus exchange in the world." Look out, West Coast Institute of Virus Research!

Did the anti-virus industry have a stroke? You bet it did. But even Richard Ford of *Virus Bulletin* grudgingly admitted in July of 1994 that Ludwig's CD-ROM "really [was] a good virus collection."[1] of Footnote

In 1994, the actual viruses in the wild bore no relation to what was considered cool in the virus underground. There were no common viruses on the loose that bore much similarity to any of

---

1 Public post by *Virus Bulletin* editor Richard Ford in Compuserve's National Computer Security Association special interest group, July 14, 1994. Subject: Virus CD-ROM.

the programs included in phalcon/SKISM's *40 Hex* magazine. Natas had been published in *40 Hex* and got away in Mexico, but no one was copying Priest's programming style even though examples of it had been spread around since 1992 with the publication of the Satan Bug. Another coveted program on the virus exchanges in the United States was the Gingerbread Man, a stealthy program and master boot record infector from Australia. It was a hot trade in the underground but it wasn't going anywhere in the real world. Perhaps if the anti-virus industry would send some press releases about Gingerbread Man to some journalists, though?

The viruses with the most staying power in the wild in mid-1994, according to informal figures put together by Bill Arnold of IBM's Anti-virus development team,[2] were:

FORM	44%
Cansu	6% (*aka* V-sign or Sigalit)
Stoned	4%
Michelangelo	3%
Noint	3%
Joshi	2%
Bouncing Ball	1% (*aka* Ping Pong)
Nov17	1% (the most common file infector)
Flip	1% (a file and master boot record infector)
1813	1% (*aka* Jerusalem)
1701	1% (*aka* Cascade-1701)
1575	1% (*aka* Green Caterpillar)

These 12 viruses accounted for roughly 68 percent of all reports and all examples predated the time when the anti-virus industry began griping about the formalization of the virus underground and the trade and stockpiling of thousands of different computer viruses on easily accessed bulletin board systems. Viruses made by the Dark Avenger—"the greatest virus writer in the world"— weren't in the list. Even Priest's viruses weren't on it, although Satan Bug and Natas had proven most successful at getting press and inconveniencing others. In fact, there was nothing very special about the common viruses. They weren't a new wave of super viruses,

---

2   Public post by IBM's Bill Arnold in Compuserve's National COmputer Security Association special interest group, June 17, 1994. Subject: The "Junkie" virus.

stealthy in new and novel ways, or even polymorphic. The most successful— FORM, Cansu, Stoned, Michelangelo, Noint and Joshi—were all boot sector viruses which travelled from PC to PC in the hands of users while hitching a ride on floppy disks. Despite the advent of the information highway, the shoe-leather express was still the only 100 percent certified reliable way of transmitting live computer virus infections efficiently. It was hard to picture how the arrest of Black Baron, Apache Warrior or any Joe Blow Virus Writer would change the statistics, either.

The virus underground and alleged evil hackers didn't even enter into a discussion of computer virus contagion undertaken in an intriguing article written by IBM researchers Jeffrey Kephart, Steve White and David Chess for the May 1993 issue of *IEEE Spectrum*. Entitled *Computers and Epidemiology*, the article unveiled research in which the investigators had tried to create synthetic models of computer virus propagation based upon their understanding of the spread of human disease.[3] After much hemming and hawing and some illustrations which looked interesting but didn't establish any convincing similarities between computer virus spread and the propagation of biological disease, the researchers established two points of note: (1) the Michelangelo virus affair in 1992 had been a watershed event—the scare surrounding it had resulted in a reduction of computer viruses, across the board, in the wild as consumers and computer systems managers rushed about, bought software and scanned their computers, disposing of everything that was uncovered; and (2) unlike human disease, infection by one computer virus can confer immunity to all.

The article also refuted one of the older theories of computer virus epidemiology, developed in 1990 by anti-virus software developer Peter Tippett, which predicted computerized disaster if current conditions went uncorrected.[4] Tippett's theory assumed exponential multiplication of computer viruses coupled to worldwide uniform sharing of infected files and diskettes.

---

3 Jeffrey Kephart, Steve WHite and David Chess, "Computers and Epidemiology", *IEEE Spectrum*, May, 1993
4 Peter Tippett, "The Kinetics of computer virus replication", *FoundationWare*, March, 1990.

You could think of uniform sharing as what results when you pour a droplet of hot water into a glass of water at room temperature. The molecules of warm water in the droplet, moving faster than their neighbors at room temperature, start bumping into molecules adjacent to them. As the different molecules collide, the faster—moving ones are damped by the cooler, or slower—moving molecules, passing on energy in the process. These molecules are now moving a little faster, but not as quickly as the original sample from the hot droplet, and they collide with cooler molecules as the cycle repeats with diminishing intensity until the entire glass of water is a uniform temperature once again, perhaps slightly warmer than before, depending upon a number of other factors I won't go into here.

Applying the idea of uniform sharing to computer viruses, one person would spread an infected disk to another, who might produce three infected disks or more on his computer, which in turn, would be passed on to as many people or more in an unending cascade until everyone in the world had received an infected computer disk, spreading the virus in a disastrous manner. Common sense indicates that this was a pretty simplistic assumption, good for scaring people, but not much else. This was apparently exactly what Tippett used it for, as he infrequently aired ideas for model legislation to regulate virus writing, one example of which appeared in David Stang's July 1992 issue of *Virus News and Reviews*, just before it ceased publication.

The anti-virus industry also kept trying to come up with new ways to certify their products. The statistics John McAfee used to discredit Microsoft Anti-virus came from Patricia Hoffman's VSUM virus database. For years, Hoffman had been compiling an ever-growing hypertext reader filled with the names of every virus which had been turned over to her. Anyone in the on-line world could quickly find a copy, VSUM's distribution was so successful. But the CARO researchers constantly criticized Hoffman's technical expertise, making jokes about the errors that peppered VSUM's virus descriptions. And they insisted that she was too close to John McAfee, that her virus collection was his collection, and that any certification testing she performed and published in VSUM was always cooked to favor McAfee Associates.

Invariably, others tried to provide certification testing of anti-virus software, but the industry could never escape from criticism that testing was always performed under the influence of particular vendors, rather than independently. From time to time vendors would perform tests just to obtain results they could use to hit competitors over the head as uncomprehending consumers looked on. One such example occurred immediately after S&S International had raised the alarm over the SMEG viruses.

Annoyed over S&S International's advertising in special interest forums devoted to anti-virus software on Compuserve, Tjark Auerbach, a German vendor of the anti-virus scanner AVScan, snidely provided his own counter-advertising.

"Here is my comparison between current av products regarding some polymorphic viruses," wrote Auerbach. "Some weeks ago, I read a blatant ad from a UK based program specialist—whatever this might be—over in VIRUSFORUM. To bring things to an end, here are the results of the comparison he triggerd [sic]." Auerbach then provided his results: the number of properly identified SMEG viruses detected in a sample volume of 53,000—that's right, 53,000—SMEG-infected files which he'd assembled.

The results, condensed, were presented as follows, with the numbers representing viruses MISSED in a sampling of 53,000 of the two program types, COM and EXE, which the SMEG viruses infected (the larger the number, the POORER the performance with 53,000 equivalent to no scanning results):

Integrity Master 2.22a

SMEG.Pathogen	COM	18
	EXE	17
SMEG.Queeg	COM	15
	EXE	17

Thunderbyte Scan 6.20

SMEG.Pathogen	COM	710
	EXE	4
SMEG.Queeg	COM	1585
	EXE	1674

Frisk Skulason's F-Prot 2.12

SMEG.Pathogen	COM	53000
	EXE	53000
SMEG.Queeg	COM	53000
	EXE	53000

Eugene Kaspersky's Antivirus Toolkit (Database 15.MAR.94)

SMEG.Pathogen	COM	53000
	EXE	53000
SMEG.Queeg	COM	53000
	EXE	53000

Norton Anti-virus 3.0 (Database 1.MAY.94 30a07)

SMEG.Pathogen	COM	53000
	EXE	53000
SMEG.Queeg	COM	53000
	EXE	53000

Central Point Anti-virus 2.1

SMEG.Pathogen	COM	53000
	EXE	53000
SMEG.Queeg	COM	53000
	EXE	53000

McAfee Associates SCAN 2.0.1

SMEG.Pathogen	COM	53000
	EXE	53000
SMEG.Queeg	COM	53000
	EXE	53000

Sophos SWEEP 2.61 (another United Kingdom-based company)

SMEG.Pathogen	COM	899
	EXE	849
SMEG.Queeg	COM	914
	EXE	866

Microsoft Anti-virus with DOS 6.2

SMEG.Pathogen	COM	53000
	EXE	53000
SMEG.Queeg	COM	53000
	EXE	53000

AVScan 1.55 (Tjark Auerbach's program, of course)

SMEG.Pathogen	COM	0
	EXE	0
SMEG.Queeg	COM	0
	EXE	0

Solomon's FindVirus (the company Auerbach was in a rhubarb with)

SMEG.Pathogen	COM	331/6000 extrapolated to 2924/53000
	EXE	332/6000 extrapolated to 2933/53000
SMEG.Queeg	COM	381/6000 extrapolated to 3366/53000
	EXE	406/6000 extrapolated to 3586/53000

(Note: 10 hours were needed to scan 6000 files, final results in approximately three days)

IBM AntiVirus/DOS 1.04J

SMEG.Pathogen	COM	53000
	EXE	53000
SMEG.Queeg	COM	53000
	EXE	53000

Auerbach's results, in addition to being a pointed-stick-in-the-eye aimed at Alan Solomon's FindVirus, weren't even derived from good experimental design if you looked at them from a scientific standpoint. In fact, they were essentially meaningless.

At the time Auerbach performed his test, the SMEG viruses were not only new, they were rare—not present in the United States. So it was unsurprising that few of the American vendors, with the exception of the Florida-based Integrity Master, detected them. There certainly was a lot wrong with the Norton, Central Point and Microsoft anti-virus programs, but you couldn't fault them for not having yet released versions of their software which attempted to look for such a new set of viruses. In light of that, operating the software on a collection of 53,000 infected files was completely superfluous grandstanding. Without asking competing vendors, Auerbach could have empirically determined the viruses hadn't been included in these products by testing a handful of samples. A few seconds of testing and a 100 percent miss rate against as few as ten infected files would have been plenty.

Nevertheless, these were the kinds of tests vendors attempted to surprise each other with. Get a new virus, one which you knew a hated competitor didn't have a copy of, run the competitor's software over a ridiculous number of programs infected by the same virus, and report the results in a public forum. Contrived certifications like these were supposed to provide a service to the consumer. Indeed.

One thing absent from this book is detailed discussion on the ethics of computer viruses. It didn't seem necessary, since the anti-virus industry already had no shortage of people ready to deliver long, preachy treatises on the subject of computer ethics to journalists, their own publications and corporate organs. Far better to rely upon them than look for anything of this nature in *The Virus Creation Labs*. But bear in mind this is the same industry that hired a virus writer to derive commercial advantage from the minor calamity his virus had caused in a foreign city. It is the same industry whose members like Vesselin Bontchev, Joe Hirst, Fridrik Skulason and others had allowed their early disassemblies and analyses of virus source code to go to anyone who wanted them, with the result that they wound up as part of the high-quality seed crop which started the first virus exchanges operated by American teenagers. It is the same industry that sanctioned the existence of moles like Gerhard Maier, solely to engage in *sub rosa* trades of viruses with the same underground denizens the industry set up as whipping boys and boogeymen in the popular press.

Ethics in the anti-virus/virus world were frequently plastic, reflected Tim Caton, the sysop of the Dark Coffin bulletin board system. Where economic interest and computer ethics intersected in this world, high-minded ideals were scarce. Ultimately, it was only the dollar, and professional reputations—if they could be hooked to profits—that mattered. The purity of Priest's single-minded approach to computer virus programming was almost inspirational by comparison. He was no hypocrite! When discussion of the ethics of destructive computer viruses came up, Priest either kept his mouth shut or let out a short laugh. Priest was a computer virus programming machine running on full automatic. If you tried to harness it, you did so at your own peril.

Of course, the virus underground was hardly filled with noblemen. Many were profane, insulting and predatory by nature. Others would deal with the anti-virus industry if they could work the angles to their advantage. We've also read of those who concocted elaborate and contorted rationalizations centered on the cracked idea that writing more viruses was actually of benefit to the consumer, because it made anti-virus programmers work harder. And there were always a few doing their damnedest to booby-trap the software of people unfortunate enough to be in their neighborhood of cyberspace. If there was any solace to be had in this brutal reality, it was in the realization that while there may have been quite a few with the will to screw up the computers of others, there were many less who had the determination and technical skill to keep at it pathologically until it really hurt.

Our little journey through some of the darker warrens and sewers of cyberspace has not been without its good points. While Alan Solomon may have pursued petty computer vandals with more zeal than appropriate, or unfairly aided and abetted the bushwhacking of Kim Clancy, there could be no argument that his software, unlike that of many of his charlatan competitors, actually worked. The Solomon Anti-virus Toolkit could do one helluva number on computer viruses. Certainly, not all the anti-virus experts were money-mad cockroaches, dangerously incompetent corporate finks peddling snake-oil or cartoon-like pseudo-scientists addicted to confabulated bragging and artifice. Some minded their own business and labored quietly at providing some quantity of competent service to their buyers. But that still left too many loudmouths and swindlers. It was time for the skeptical to don the steel-toed boots of retribution and take a run at planting a few where it really hurt.

And not all virus writers were scum of the earth. In fact, a number were quite interesting people—hardly caricatures of plotting evil. You had to respect the sheer cussedness, entrepreneurial imagination and frank unwillingness to compromise of John Buchanan. Nowhere Man had the sense to recognize when a good idea was mined to the max and it was time to leave the playing field to others. Stormbringer never stopped in his quest for the good virus. And Priest—well, you could always count on him to write good code, no matter if it was the next Natas virus or the cure for it.

Afterword

Hold it, I'm not done yet.

Because of the ugly, controversial nature of computer viruses, perforce I've run roughshod over the term "hacker" in *The Virus Creation Labs.* Such was not my intent, but there are always going to be a number of extremely irritated nabobs who will complain I've done nothing for an image that has already been dragged through the muck by the popular media. The original hackers were good people, or something like that, not two-timing, virus-writing rats, will be one possible cry. Count on the nutso idealists to make it, but if you look closely at *The Virus Creation Labs,* I'm sure you will see that some of the characters herein had many, many good points. If you don't see them, so be it, and if there are those who think I set out to make all hackers look like creeps, I can live with it, even though it's far from true.

And there are those who will complain because I've covered some of the darker areas of cyberspace, without offering much of the happy, fuzzy, intellectually satisfying, democracy- returned-to-the-people, everyone reborn, free-information-is-power, virtual-this-virtual-that mental crackerjack-with-plastic-toy-in-packet pizazz favored by other reporters on the beat. But what did you think this would be, a walk in the park? *Caveat emptor.*

Closely linked with this is the decision not to name quite a few of the characters in the book. Where you find real names, the people involved had already given me the OK or become so entangled in the public record, there was no point in trying to obscure their identities. As for those who preserved their handles, consider for a moment how people in your neck of the woods commonly react to the idea of computer viruses or those suspected of programming them. Might there be one or two in the bunch who would make it their personal business to invade the privacy of a complete stranger or make nasty telephone calls to employers, friends, parents, acquaintances or teachers with the sole aim of filling the head of anyone who would listen with unsubstantiated, spittle-spraying-from-the-mouth accusations? Remember, virus writing isn't even close to being a crime in the U.S., no matter how many might wish it so. That could change, but not today.

It would be remiss if I didn't mention *The Crypt Newsletter*. *The Crypt Newsletter* started out as a publication where I could be Joe Virus Writer. Early issues of it from two years ago show why it was just the ticket to ride into the underground. The newsletter was ugly, mean and direct. Its banner for the first five months or so was:

```
**************************************************
Another festive, info-glutted, tongue-in-cheek
training manual provided solely for the enter-
tainment of the virus programmer, casual by-
stander or PC hobbyist interested in the
particulars of cybernetic data replication
and/or destruction.
**************************************************
```

It published some of the first examples of Virus Creation Laboratory and PS-MPC viruses.

The Crypt Newsletter regularly published virus code submitted by Stormbringer, myself, members of the Trident virus-writing group, Kohntark—who for a time was the whimsically named Crypt Entropic Systems Editor—and Nikademus, a college student who enjoyed writing viruses which interfered with or deleted anti-virus software. (Kohntark was one of the first to realize how a ridiculously small piece of code could be used to disarm the Central Point and Microsoft Anti-virus's memory-installed sentry. Or was it Ralf Brown? I saw the same thing in the Virus/Anti-virus chapter of his *PC Interrupts* programming reference.[1]) Crypt also published detailed articles on the CIA's induction methods for would-be spies, the spy-satellite-flying National Reconnaissance Office, the

hantavirus plague in the summer of 1993 and the virtual unemploy-
ment boom affecting many American programers, among others.

The Crypt Newsletter and its editor knew the virus underground
intimately, enjoying a first-name basis with the characters in *The
Virus Creation Labs*. Have I annoyed the pansies in the audience
enough, do you think?

---

1 Ralf Brown and James Kyle, *PC Interrupts*, Addison-Wesley, 1994.

Appendix A:
The Trident Virus Research Group

Although *The Virus Creation Labs* focuses on the United States, mention of the Trident virus-writing group and its members wends its way in and out of the narrative. Simply, this was because the Dutch hacking group encompassed some of the most interesting and accomplished virus writers in the underground.

It was Masud Khafir of Trident who had programed the Trident Polymorphic Engine and other programs like the Cruncher virus. Cruncher was a program inspired by Dr. Fred Cohen's lectures and notes on productive, or servant viruses. Theoretically, it was easy to imagine a replicating program designed to compress programs on an infected machine. Khafir's Cruncher virus shrank infected programs using a technique employed by a compression tool known as DIET. DIET was a popular piece of software written by a programmer named Teddy Matsumoto. Cruncher made DIET ambulatory. The virus would install itself in memory and infect other programs it found suitable for "crunching" using the DIET method, shrinking them in the process and freeing up more data storage space on the infected computer. It was Khafir's attempt at a productive virus and it raised quite a bit of controversy in anti-virus and virus circles, even more when the Microsoft Anti-virus began returning false indications of Cruncher infections in

DIET compressed programs because its programmers had mistakenly zeroed in on one of the DIET-specific strings of code. An extensive set of interviews with the Trident group was published in the February 1994 issue of an underground electronic magazine from Sweden called *Insane Reality*. Despite the fearsome, off-putting name, the editors of *Insane Reality*, The Unforgiven and Metal Militia, had managed to put together some of the most lucid and intriguing interviews conducted with virus authors to date. The magazine, if you can find it anymore, is worth seeking out. But even if you can't, portions of the Trident interviews are republished here with only slight embellishments for the sake of clarity. If there ever was a virus writing group deserving of being called independent researchers, it was these guys.

Interview with Masud Khafir

Insane Reality [IR]: Give me a short description of who you are!
Masud Khafir [MK]—I am Masud Khafir, virus writer; age: twenty-something; country: The Netherlands. That's about all that I want to reveal about my identity.
IR: Where did you get your handle, Masud Khafir?
MK: 'Masud' is a common name in the Middle East. I chose [it] in the spring of 1991, when the Kurd rebellion in Iraq was active. Their leader was Masud Barzani. There are more rebel leaders with [the] name: Masud Rajavi, leader of the Iranian Mujahedin e Khalq and Ahmad Shah Masud, [an] Afghan rebel leader. 'Khafir' is a word I once found in the dictionary. It's Arab and is a rude word for non-Muslims. In the South African language it's 'kaffir' and means 'nigger'. In Holland it is 'kaffer' and is used for calling someone an idiot. I found it a funny word, because of its strange history.
IR: When did you discover the world of computers?
MK: A long time ago. My first computer was a Commodore-64. That was about ten years ago.
IR: How did you come to write viruses?
MK: It started when I got a virus from a friend. I disassembled [it] and after that, I was wondering if I could write one myself. At the same time I started reading the virus areas on Fidonet and it

was there that I read of Todor Todorov's Virus exchange BBS [in Bulgaria]. I was very curious about [it] . . . so I called a few times.

IR: What do you see as positive and negative aspects of the virus scene?

MK: I think that the attitude towards the AV community is sometimes a bit too hostile. I see it more like a chess game. They are our opponents, but we don't have to be enemies. Many of them are just nice people. But, of course, the same is true for the other side. Some of them just hate us. What I don't like is the negative image of the scene—that adolescent rebellious attitude and creating an image of oneself as evil and dangerous. But that's just my personal opinion. This also means that I don't like destructive viruses.

IR: What is the Trident group's goal?

MK: I think the main goal is to keep in touch with each other. There's not big cooperation on writing viruses. Everybody does their own thing.

IR: You've programed a lot of polymorphic things, and one of these is the Trident Polymorphic Engine. What comments have you received about it?

MK: Well, various . . . it got quite some attention in the virus/antivirus world. It's also one of the things that made the name Trident known.

IR: Will you continue to "upgrade" TPE, or is it a finished project?

MK: TPE is now finished. The first versions all had bugs. I thought that version 1.3 would be the last one, but it still had a small bug. Version 1.4 seems to be OK, as far as I know. Besides, I don't think I would want to put out a new version again, anymore.

IR: How many different viral mutations can it produce?

MK: I have no idea. Enough, I think. The most important thing is that the decryptors of the TPE cannot be found with wildcard scan strings. That's the main idea behind polymorphism.

IR: Even though polymorphic engines are a great thing, not many people seem to use them. Do you have any theory why this might be so?

MK: I think most people just want to make their own, rather than use someone else's product. And, maybe, because anti-virus writers have been quite successful in finding ways to detect them.

IR: Which is the best polymorphic engine around today?

MK: It's hard to say. I've seen several of them, but I haven't done a real close study on any. Each of them has its strong and weak points, I think. Of course there are not only the engines, but also a lot of other polymorphic viruses, like [the Washburn viruses], Maltese Amoeba, Uruguay . . . TPE started this way, too, [with Giraffe]. Some of these viruses are just as advanced as the engines. But none of those engines and viruses are perfect. For every one of them, the AV people have found a solution.

IR: What viruses have you written?

MK: The most known: Gotcha, 7th Son, Little Brother, Pogue, CoffeeShop, WinVir, TPE, Cruncher, PlayGame.

IR: Which one was the hardest?

MK: Probably the first, Gotcha. WinVir and Cruncher were quite hard, too.

IR: Is there any sort of law enforcement organization trying to hunt Trident down?

MK: Perhaps . . . There is a new law [in Holland] against various computer crimes since [March 1 1993]. Writing a virus is not illegal. Distributing viruses, in any way, can be illegal. The law is not very clear [on] this. If we, as writers, exchange viruses amongst each other, that could, perhaps, be interpreted as illegal. Last year another guy in Holland was arrested for hacking, and although he hasn't been convicted for anything, yet, law enforcement has been quite tough on him. So they certainly can make your life hard if they want to.

IR: Which virus-group or programers do you admire?

MK: Of course, Dark Avenger was one of the best, maybe THE best. He often introduced new techniques. I also admire Dark Angel from phalcon/SKISM. But to be honest, I don't often take a deep look at other viruses anymore these days.

IR: Which country has best virus-writers today?

MK: I haven't heard anything from Bulgaria in a long time. Sometimes I'm nostalgic for the time when Bulgaria was the virus center of the world. Today it's probably the USA, because it's the biggest country in the West. I think it's strange we don't hear that much about Russia.

IR: Give me your opinion of the anti-virus industry in a few lines.

MK: We need them. I think every virus writer uses anti-virus programs. It is nice when a virus can be smarter than the current anti-virus software, but it would be scary if they couldn't find a solution for [some program]. But it's a shame that some anti-virus people hate us.

IR: Which anti-virus program do think are the best and why?

MK: I like Thunderbyte Scan a lot, mainly for its heuristic features. And it's fast. F-Prot is best in identifying viruses and it's very user friendly. I also like Eugene Kasperky's Anti-virus Professional from Russia. Sometimes it's a bit slow, but it is very powerful. It also has a very nice info section.

IR: Do you have any advice for aspiring virus writers?

MK: Take a good look at other viruses and [their] source codes. Try to understand their weak and strong points. Test your stuff before you give it away, because it's a shame to have dozens of bug-fix updates for the same virus. Do it for the fun of it, and not to cause other people trouble. And try to be original.

Interview with John Tardy

IR: Where did you get your handle, John Tardy?

JT: In the beginning of time, I was fascinated by certain death metal groups like Deicide and Obituary. The lead singer of Obituary is John Tardy. I wanted to adapt his name into the underground. If you know the first group, you know my handle when I was younger, Glenn Benton . . .

IR: How did you come to be a virus writer?

JT: That's a nice, confusing question. When I first was struck by a virus myself, I was convinced of the menace of [them]. I wanted to kill these things that ruined my PC. So I wanted to write a scanner or another anti-virus toolkit. I contacted several [people] in The Netherlands, including the author of Thunderbyte Scan, but they pulled me off. I wasn't trustworthy, and so on . . . Then I read a document from Vesselin Bontchev, about the virus exchange BBSes. You could only get a virus from them if you wrote one yourself, he said. So I did . . .

IR: What's Trident's goal?

JT: Hmmm, that's not really an easy one. . . We want to be known—which is now the case—but we all have personal goals, too. I want to have the fuzz cleared away about the anti-virus writers. If they had been more open to me, I wouldn't have made a virus or even founded Trident. I would be a researcher, then . . . I can't do that now, because of my history as a virus writer, so I'll have to go on and on and on. Blame them! A cartel isn't good!

IR: Who are the leaders of Trident?

JT: Hmmm, let them speak for themselves. I am only the founder, but not the best programmer of the bunch. Bit Addict is surely the best and Masud Khafir is in second place, but we are not used to things like "ratings," because we share the same interest.

IR: Which virus have you written?

JT: There are many . . . I guess around sixty or so. But the most well known are Circus Clusters, Servant and OW 0-10. Some other viruses, like Deicide, are known as mine, but they're not with this name and I don't want to be associated with the old [ones] anymore.

IR: Which one was the hardest to write?

JT: Circus Clusters was an interesting experiment, and I had a little trouble making the virus stable, which you could see in an old *Crypt Newsletter*. I made it up for [them] in a newer one.

IR: What do you think about the laws against hacking, phreaking and virus-writing that have arrived lately?

JT: It's a very sad business. What I want to do on MY computers is no one's business. If I want to release a virus on my system, who's to say I may not? And giving source code to someone to see how a virus works, is THAT illegal? They're just plain texts! Other people compile and release them; it's not my responsibility. They can also watch and say "This is nice" and then throw it away. The laws in The Netherlands are vague and not very specific. These laws would also make virus researchers illegal, if they send samples to each other.

IR: Do you think these laws are more bark than bite?

JT: I think they could be a real threat, not only for us, but for censoring the whole scene. That would be very bad. I am not so worried for myself, but more about the fact that the anti-virus business has become a very awful thing with CARO, which wanted to set up a murky database and hunt people down.

IR: What do you think when newspapers characterize hackers as nerds?

JT: I have a good laugh at them. I just wear hair curlers in my beard and a condom on my nose in order to ward off radiation. Hello, Dr. Joseph Popp! No, let them think their way, I think my way.

Interview with Crom-Cruach

IR: Describe yourself!

CC: Hacker, phreaker, raver, freak and stoner . . .

IR: Where did you get your handle?

CC: Crom-Cruach is the ancient Irish supreme Wormgod.

IR: How did you come to write viruses?

CC: Some years ago the media started to hype the New Danger. I was able to find a copy of Brain and Burger viruses, debugged them to death, and made a simple direct-action .COM infector which was never released . . . probably wiped out with one of my zillion hard drive crashes.

IR: What part(s) of the underground do you think are counter-productive?

CC: The destructive part. I still can't figure why people smart enough to make a nice virus are unable to see that they harm both foes and friends with it. Also, part of the underground still parties a lot, but doesn't do anything against the continuing [diminution] of their rights.

IR: What's Trident's goal?

CC: Throw parties once in a while—ahem—create and divide chaos?

IR: How is Trident organized?

CC: It's not. Anarchy to the bone.

IR: Have you ever thought of publishing some sort of electronic magazine?

CC: I wrote a hypertext *Hitchhiker's Guide to Viruses* and stopped when I was 90 percent done. When I've got time, I'll finish it. Someday . . .

IR: Which viruses have you written?

CC: I haven't released that many. Little Mess, Horns of Jericho, Weirdo and Cheeba were the only ones, I believe. I mostly write programs showing a specific hole in system protection, I rarely build an entire virus around it.

IR: Which one was the hardest to write?

CC: I can't tell. I always write one because I want to try something new ... Little Mess spreads itself through Telix Salt-scripts and I had to figure out that format. Horns of Jericho ate its way through Thunderbyte Scan's .AVR files, if you can still remember when Thunderbyte used them.

IR: What do you think about newspapers describing us as nerds?

CC: Who cares about the opinions of somebody studying something this big for one single day?! I couldn't care less about those who believe everything written in newspapers.

IR: Would you feel guilty if one of your viruses damaged computers at a hospital?

CC: Yes. Does this really need an explanation? I always try to make my viruses as compatible as possible, and surely don't make destructive ones. Sheesh, it is way more difficult to make something really non-destructive.

IR: Describe the anti-virus industry in a few lines.

CC: Nerds wearing anoraks and such. Or, a bunch of would-be cover girls eager to attract the public's attention, smiling holy, and in the meantime kicking each other hard below the camera field. [Winks.]

IR: Do you know of any new virus techniques coming in the near future?

CC: I'm pretty sure the PowerPC will give virus authors a wide scale of new possibilities.

Appendix B:
Do Virus-Writers Hose Themselves?

The question is occasionally asked, "How do virus-writers keep from infecting themselves?" The short answer is, "They don't."

However, sometimes they write about it with remarkable candor, which is something you will never see from a corporation or institution that has suffered a virus attack.

Again, the underground journalists from Sweden, The Unforgiven and Metal Militia, reported on their encounter with one of Priest's destructive viruses in the electronic pages of *Insane Reality* magazine.

Some of the original copy has been edited for clarity.

The Predator Virus Strikes!

by The Unforgiven

Well, first off, this article is kinda "embarrassing." But after all, we believe in democracy, information-freedom, and a society without censorship. That's the reason I included this little report. I'll start from the beginning, so pay attention please!

The whole thing started when I leeched a file from the excellent bulletin board, FireDoom Systems. The file was some sort of credit card number calculator, which was described as supporting Visa, Mastercard and American Express. I thought that if it worked— against all odds—it would be an easy way to get hardware and decrease phone bills. If it didn't, it would be the perfect way of getting our Ravage virus a bit spread out, so all the "illegal" card abusers had a hard time removing it.

I hate to say this, but Phalcon/SKISM had "calculated" exactly the same thoughts. Yes, the "ware" was infected, but not with Ravage, with the Predator virus.

I closed down my system right away, and turned it on some seconds later, cleaning the computer's memory. "Haha!" I thought, and removed the calculator from my hard disk, thinking that if it was a virus or not, I was free from it. I was DEAD WRONG! This virus was HARD to get rid of! Trust me on that!

First of all, the virus had absolutely no bugs, and I didn't notice that my computer was under attack by this "shitty" . . . little destructive piece of code. The virus was pretty big—2448 bytes— but since it used lots of stealth functions, like file-size change hiding, I didn't noticed it until it was too late.

The first time I noticed Predator, was when I looked at the new video display program, which was to be included in this issue . . . the file had grown, and would not run.

Metal Militia called me, and I gave him my copy of the infected program. Metal Militia opened that file, and "Ha, ha, ha, very funny," he said. He was looking at a text string in the program: "Predator virus #2 (c) 1993 Priest—Phalcon/Skism".

He thought I was making some bad joke. I told him that I wasn't, and after some time he believed me.

The first thing Predator did with my computer was to copy itself to the partition sector. It then becomes resident when you restart the computer. When resident it will infect .COM and .EXE programs, which are executed or copied.

The virus also plays around with the file allocation table, thus making it destructive. It . . . randomly puts together some parts of files placed on a sector with other files. For example, I wound up with a combined .EXE program spliced with some dull text file.

Predator has stealth functions and will spoof attempts to look into infected programs as well as the infected partition sector with images that indicate the virus is not there. First, you will not see that a file is infected . . . I looked at the partition sector and couldn't see the virus, so I thought . . . not a boot virus. PUH!

But now, I know better . . .

Metal Militia started cleaning his infected computer by using the "SMASH" logic bomb released by Phalcon/SKISM. I called my friend Raver, knowing that he had written some sort of "Remove" program. I started it up, and it deleted all my executables! I thought that I finally was rid of this nasty bastard! DEAD WRONG AGAIN!

What I didn't know, was that Predator infected the partition sector as well as programs.

I thought, "Oh, shit! Now we'll never release the second issue of our magazine. Gee, what a sin!"

Heh-heh . . . it was justice for all . . . and this was my punishment for all "bad" things I had caused the computerworld.

Anyway, I copied some programs from Raver's computer, mostly Norton Utilities stuff, like the the Norton Disk Doctor. I started up the program, and it told me immediately that something was wrong with the partition sector. The program continued its work. Finally, I was rid of it!

I'm really sorry if my diagnosis is full of rubbish. It can't be helped!

I didn't analyze the virus, and didn't really care about all the functions in it, since it was extremely hard to clean.

Well, this was the 100 percent true story about the Predator virus. My mind is kinda split about the whole virus scene right now. I surely adore Priest for doing this virus. But at the same time I hate him! He's caused us—especially me—LOTS of TROUBLE! And what can he say in his defense? Not very much! There isn't any potential risk that someone just stole Predator from his computer and started spreading it. Nah. He has probably written it for spreading and for evil purposes only.

Just like we do.

So, isn't this just some sort of double moral standard? Yes, I can't figure out anything else to call it. Anyway, now I'm clean, except that I must re-install all my programs, and search for all the great ones that I've lost. It's gonna be some sort of boring weekend!

What have I then learned? Lots of things! First: make backups and a virus, destructive ones, will hardly cause you any trouble at all. Second: Priest is a hell of a coder. I hate to admit that. Third: If virus writers come to the more destructive things, this will be some sort of inspiration to writing better viruses.

But even if we've learned some things from this, I can't say it was a pleasure. It ain't phun to learn the hard way!

Acknowledgments

The Virus Creation Labs couldn't have been completed without the help of a number of interesting and clever people. First, there is Mark Ludwig, a publisher and editor who respects the need to tell a story completely unvarnished. Nowhere Man, John Buchanan, Tim Caton, Kim Clancy and Dave Goldsmith were continuously generous with their time and opened their memories and files unflinchingly during the research stage of my journey. My thanks to the people who run the Hell Pit for letting me hang about and get my hands on just about any text file or program I wanted for the better part of two years. The computer security areas of the National Institute of Standards and Technology BBS has nothing over the Hell Pit!

Jim Thomas at *Computer underground Digest* deserves a high five for brief hand-holding, which he probably forgets, and allowing his publication to be a proving ground for some of the preliminary work which wound up forming the basis for a bit of the more inflammatory material in *The Virus Creation Labs*. Brent Hamm provided critical background on the FIDO-net's more psychotic idiosyncracies, which lent itself to chapter four just as it was being written. It was investigative digging on the fly! Enjoy your complimentary copy, Brent. Thanks to Paul Melka for providing the occasional clipping service. Hats off to Frank Tirado at the U.S. Department of Agriculture and Jim Lipshultz of the Drug Enforcement Agency for service above and beyond.

Kohntark provided spot technical services for *The Crypt Newsletter* which were carried over, in one form or another, to the book.

He also hipped me to a real word-processing program, as opposed to Microsoft's EDIT which I'd used to plague the innocent on a regular basis. Michael Paris of the CriS bulletin board system in Cicero, Illinois, allowed me to be a fly-on-the-wall of the FIDO-net and NuKE-net for longer than I care to remember, hassle free. Thanks, Mike. Hans Braun and BBS Systems of San Francisco, provided free access to Usenet newsgroups of interest, another welcome development during the writing of this book. And Andy Lopez, the infamous Mr. Badger, rates a tip o'the hat for being dangerously like-minded with Urnst Kouch and providing encouragement and moral support. We'll chase them like rats across the tundra, Badger! Thompson Network Software of Marietta, Georgia, is responsible for providing me with the first anti-virus software suite which actually worked as advertised way back in February of 1992. It was called Virus-Buster then and now it's called The Doctor, but as far as I can tell it's the same program, one that opened my eyes to the differences between what most people were being told was good anti-virus software and what actually was. In this world, that's a real compliment, guys.

Last, but not least, Beth Troy for being just the right kind of computers-and-technology-hating Luddite. If on retelling, *The Virus Creation Labs* could keep her riveted, I had to be on the right track.

If you find any mistakes in *The Virus Creation Labs*, they're mine and mine alone, except when I insist otherwise.

I'll see all of you standing in the debris.

George Smith
Pasadena, July 1994

A Selected Bibliography

Burger, Ralf, *Computer Viruses and Data Protection*, Abacus: Data Becker. 1991. (Originally the English edition was called *Computer Viruses—A High Tech Disease*, but it seems to have been given a makeover in the title, perhaps to lull computing conservatives into forgetting about it. Burger's book contains Bernd Fix's disassembly of the Vienna virus as well as sections on creating viruses from batch files, mutilation of computer data and simulating horrible hardware problems with software. It remains an interesting book, particularly when you consider that a publisher agreed back in 1988 to go ahead with a project which was essentially devoted to teaching you how to administer the equivalent of computer "hot foots" to the less informed.)

Cohen, Fred, *A Short Course on Computer Viruses*, J. Wiley & Sons, 1994. (There's some math in this book which you won't understand, but since Cohen coined the term computer virus in the U.S. in 1983, it's critical you read this if you have more than a passing interest in the programs.)

Garfinkel, Simson, Daniel Weise and Steven Strassman, *The Unix-Haters Handbook*, IDG Books, 1994. (This is one very weird book which has nothing to do with computer viruses. However, it's immensely funny and Rich Salz's chapter devoted to the Usenet is one of the best things in print that describes the peculiar psychology of the on-line world, the same place with borders on Paskell Paris's FIDO-net echos and Vesselin Bontchev's comp.virus in *The Virus Creation Labs*.)

Hruska, Jan, *Computer Viruses and Anti-virus Warfare*, Ellis Horwood, 1992. (Hruska's book generated the hysteria about hackers being analogous to drug addicts, and for that it earns the Urnst Kouch categorization as the "Reefer Madness" of computer virus books. However, Hruska's book is the best on the subject authored by a software vendor, an area which includes much less editorially sound material from Alan Solomon and John McAfee, among others.)

Levy, Steven, *Hackers: Heroes of The Computer Revolution*, Anchor Press/Doubleday, 1984. (In case you were wondering where the hacker slogans about questioning authority and unrestricted flow of information come from, this is where to aim the shotgun.)

Ludwig, Mark, *The Little Black Book of Computer Viruses*, American Eagle, 1990. (Ludwig's book was a good start for me, as you can tell if you've gotten this far. If you get a copy, time how long it takes you to be declared a computing pariah in your neighborhood once you've let everyone know you're reading it.)

Mungo, Paul and Bryan Clough, *Approaching Zero: The Extraordinary Underworld of Hackers, Phreakers, Virus Writers and Keyboard Criminals*, Random House, 1992. (When this was originally published, I scoffed at it in a review for *The Crypt Newsletter*. I was wrong. I kept waiting for a better book weaving the early goings on of hackers, crackers, phreakers and virus writers together and it never appeared. While slimmer on virus material than the book jacket promises, *Approaching Zero* stays a lucid, entertaining read.)

George Smith, Ph. D., lives in southern California where he writes and edits the *Crypt Newsletter*. His doctorate is in chemistry from Lehigh University. While there, he worked on real "flesh-eating bacteria," investigating the proteins produced by the pathogen, *Vibrio vulnificus*, a microorganism which dissolves the skin, blood vessels and connective tissue of its host.

After completing post-doctoral work at the Penn State School of Medicine, Smith went to work for a newspaper in eastern Pennsylvania. After writing a series of articles in 1991 dealing with secrecy and armaments production within the military industrial complex, he was awarded a Knight Special Fellowship on "the nuts and bolts of nuclear proliferation," sponsored by New York University's Center for War Peace and the News Media, and the University of Maryland.

Since then, he has continued to write on issues in science and technology, the computer underground, and computer viruses. His *Crypt Newsletter* broke the story about the sixteen-year-old hacker's virus that took Secret Service networks off-line for three days in 1993 and was used as a primary source when the government found it had an interest in quizzing the author of the Satan Bug.

Smith has a cat named Urnst Kouch and you can e-mail him (the author, not the cat) on the internet at 70743.1711@compuserve.com.